STUDENT MADE THEMATIC MINI BOOKS

with Extension Activities to Increase Language Literacy

by Jennifer C. Freeman

Happy Reading! Jennifer C. Freeman

Incentive Publications, Inc.
Nashville, Tennessee

Illustrated by Keith H. Freeman
Cover by Marta J. Drayton
Edited by Charlotte Bosarge

ISBN 0-86530-600-1

PRINTED IN THE UNITED STATES OF AMERICA
www.incentivepublications.com

Table of Contents

Fall

Winter

Spring

Holidays

Critters

Music

Sweet Treats

Number Practice

Create Your Own Mini Book

INTRODUCTION

Purpose

The following mini books are designed for early childhood classrooms. Teachers in pre-k, kindergarten, and first grade classrooms will find the books useful. Each mini book is designed around early childhood thematic units. When used in addition to a print-rich environment, the books and activities will reinforce emerging literacy skills. The predictable texts will build reading confidence in young learners, and teachers will find them beneficial in reinforcing high frequency words, number concepts, and color words.

How to Use the Books

The books can be used in a variety of ways. Before the children make their own mini books, the teacher can read the book to the entire class. Many teachers prefer to assemble a bigger "Teacher's Copy" of each book to go along with each mini book. Introduce the book to the class by reading the "Teacher's Copy" first, then continue to read the book together during shared reading time until the end of the lesson. The entire class can create mini books as a whole group, or the mini books can be created individually. After the children have created the mini books, they can practice reading by themselves, with a partner, or in small groups. The teacher can divide the class into small groups and read and discuss the mini book throughout the theme. When the theme is over, the children take their mini books home and read them to their family. Copies of the books are left in the classroom library for children to read throughout the school year.

Extension Activities

The book also includes many useful extension activities in the areas of art, math, music, language, and science. These activities can be used in whole group settings or in learning centers. Some of the extension activities are perfect for take-home projects that the entire family can enjoy. Extension activities will encourage children to work together and include hands-on science experiments, math games, and cooking activities. Children are given opportunities to express themselves through creative art projects, songs, and movement. Thematic poems and chants expose children to an even more inspiring print-rich environment and can be used during shared reading time.

Apples! Apples! Apples!

Objectives

- ✦ Recognizing the color words in context: red, green, yellow, and blue.
- ✦ Building confidence as a reader.

Extension Activities

- ✦ Go on a field trip to an apple orchard.
- ✦ Buy a variety of different kinds of apples (for example, Golden Delicious, Red Delicious, Granny Smith, Macintosh, Gala, and Winesap). Sort the apples by size and color. Have an apple taste test where the children taste the different varieties of apples. Create a class graph where the children decide which apple they liked the best.
- ✦ Make apple prints by cutting apples in half and dipping the apple halves in paint. Make sure to cut some of the apples in half (horizontally) so they can see the star in the middle.
- ✦ Have the children make Apple Pizzas for snack. Have an apple party where they bob for apples, eat candy apples, and apple pie, and drink apple cider.
- ✦ Read the book *Ten Apples Up on Top* by Theodore LeSieg. After reading the book give the children an "Apple Friend worksheet" and have them draw ten apples on the apple friend's head. Have the children draw or glue a photograph of themselves on the apple friend's face.
- ✦ Give every child an apple tree outline and twelve pieces of Red Hot™ candies. Write the following poem on chart paper. Write different numbers in the blank and have the children put that many Red Hot™(apples) on their apple tree.

The Apple Tree

Way up high in the apple tree,

_________ little apples smiled at me.

I shook the tree just as hard as I could,

Down came the apples,

Mmmmm, they were good!

Additional Sources

- *The Seasons of Arnold's Apple Tree*
  by Gail Gibbons
  (Harcourt Brace, 1988)

- *The Apple Pie Tree*
  by Zoe Hall and Shari Halpern
  (Scholastic Trade, 1996)

- *Apples*
  by Elaine Landau
  (Children's Press, 2000)

- *Ten Apples Up on Top*
  by Theodore LeSieg
  (Random House, 1961)

- *Eating Apples*
  by Gail Saunders-Smith
  (Pebble Books, 1997)

Apples! Apples! Apples!

Name ________________________________

Yellow apples — yum.

Red apples — yum.

Green apples — yum.

Blue apples — yuk!

My favorite apple

is_______________________.

Apple Friend

Name ____________________

Apple Friend

Name ___________________________

APPLE PIZZAS

You will need:
- biscuits
- butter
- apple slices
- cinnamon
- sugar
- waxed paper
- knife
- cookie sheet

1. Spread out biscuits on waxed paper. Flatten with hand.

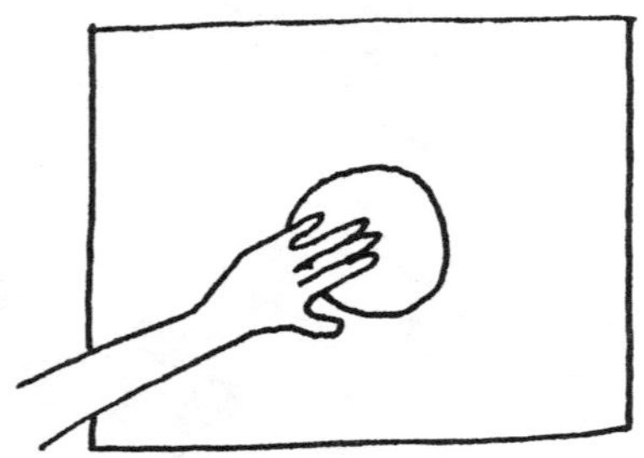

2. Spread on butter with a knife.

3. Put on apple slices.

4. Sprinkle with cinnamon and sugar.

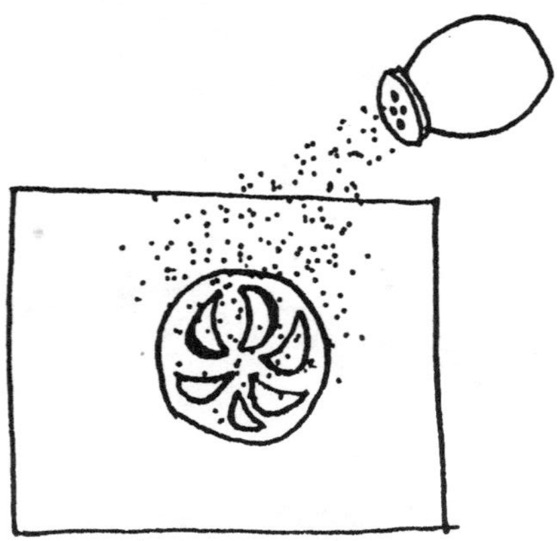

5. Bake on cookie sheet for 8–10 minutes at 450°.

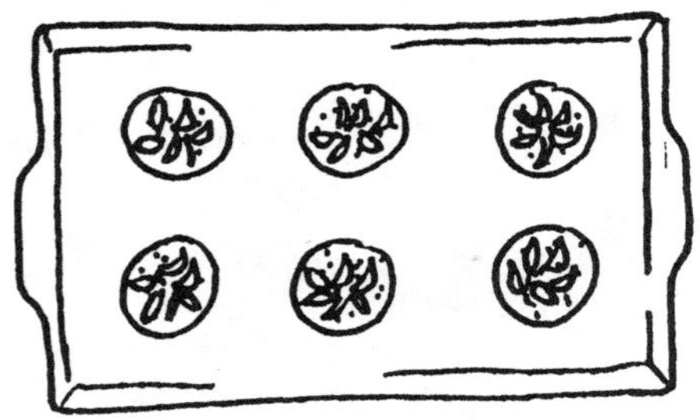

Leaves, Leaves on the Tree

Objectives

- ✦ Recognizing the color words in context: red, brown, green, yellow, and orange.
- ✦ Identifying different varieties of leaves.
- ✦ Building confidence as a reader.

Extension Activities

- ✦ Go on a nature walk and collect leaves.
- ✦ Sort collected leaves by size, shape, and color. When sorting the leaves by size have children see if the leaf is smaller or larger than his/her hand. Look for jagged and smooth outlines when sorting the leaves by shape. Have the children suggest several ways to sort the leaves.
- ✦ Create rubbings with the leaves the children collect. Provide the children with a selection of paper and writing tools.
- ✦ Observe the four seasons by adopting a tree and watching it throughout the school year. Have the children keep a "tree journal" in which they draw, record, and date the observable changes in the tree. Take photographs of the tree so the children can compare the changes.
- ✦ Have the children act like trees. Start with autumn when the leaves are falling and blowing in the wind, continue with winter when the tree is still and bare, act out spring when little buds are beginning to form, and end with summer when the tree is filled with leaves.

Additional Sources

- *Red Leaf, Yellow Leaf*
  by Lois Ehlert
  (Scholastic, 1991)

- *When Autumn Comes*
  by Robert Maas
  (Henry Holt, 1991)

- *Autumn Days*
  by Ann Schweninger
  (Penguin, 1991)

By ______________________________

---

maple

Red leaves fall.

redbud

Green leaves fall.

elm

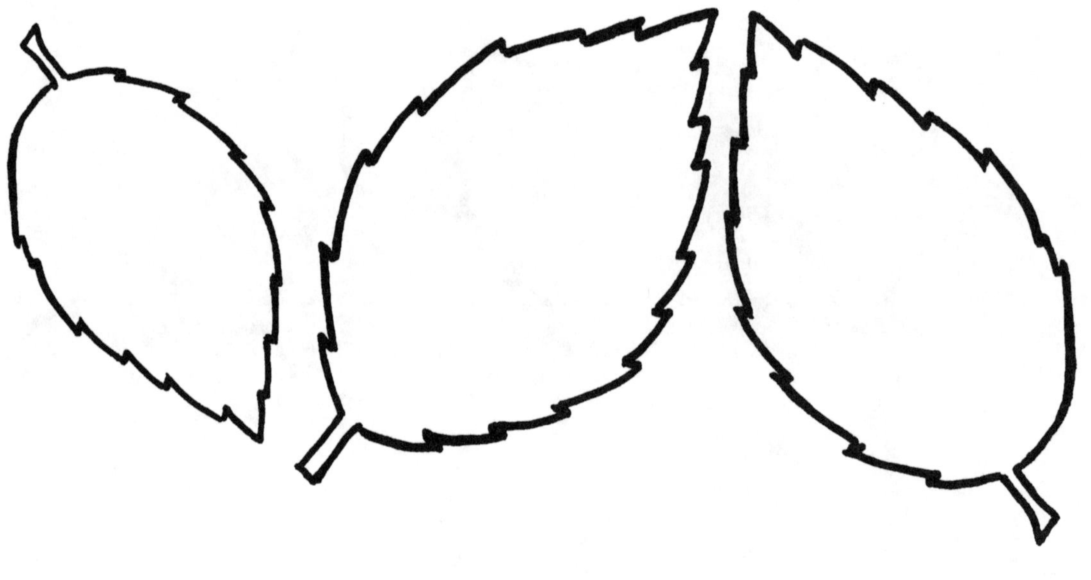

Yellow leaves fall.

oak

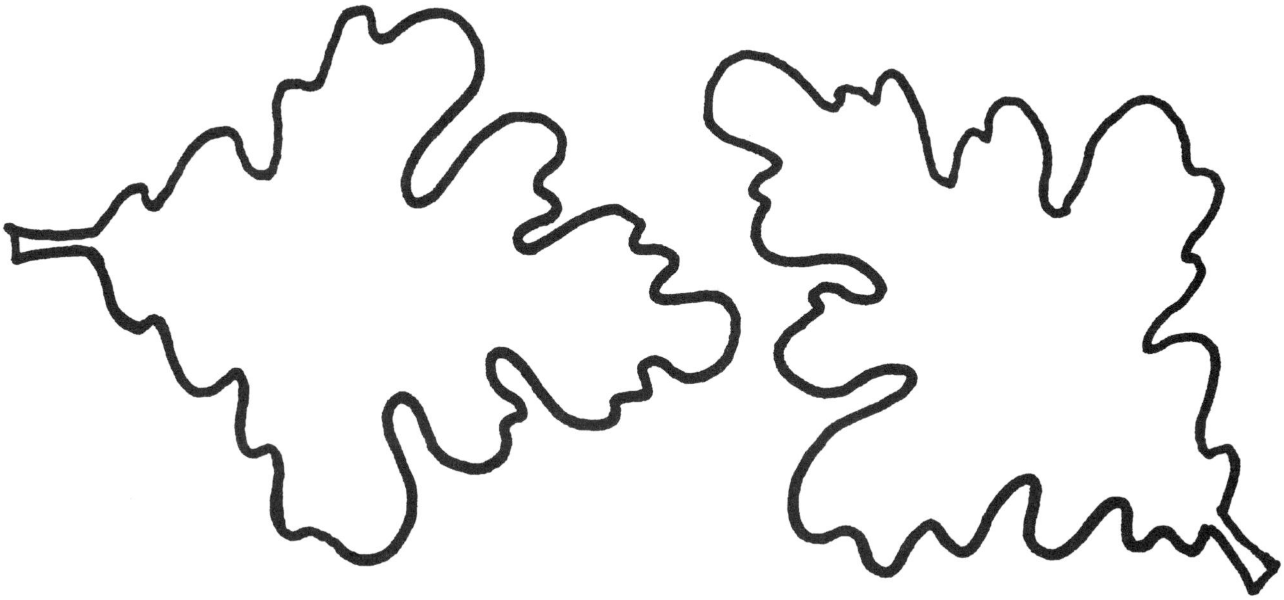

Brown leaves fall.

Leaves, leaves all set free!

ginkgo

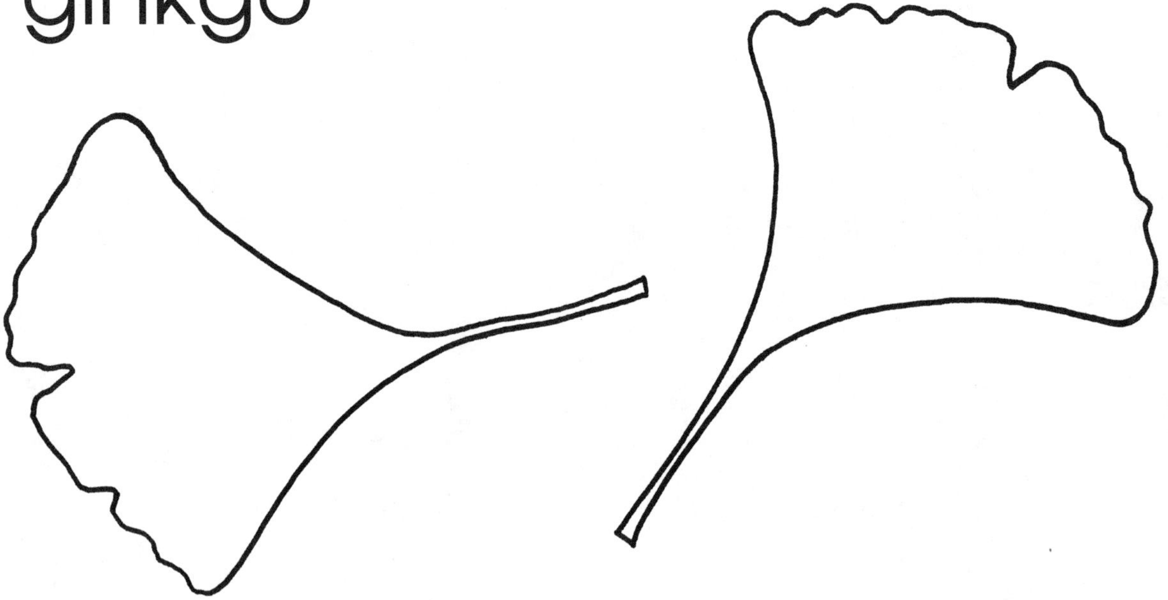

Orange leaves fall.

My favorite leaf

Our Tree

This visit was on ______________.

Here is our tree.

Leaf Sorting Name ______________________

- Sort the leaves by **jagged** or **smooth** edge.
- Cut and paste the leaves.

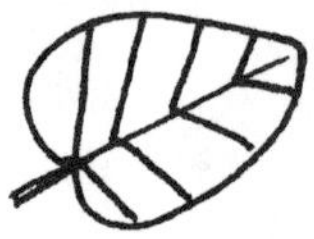	

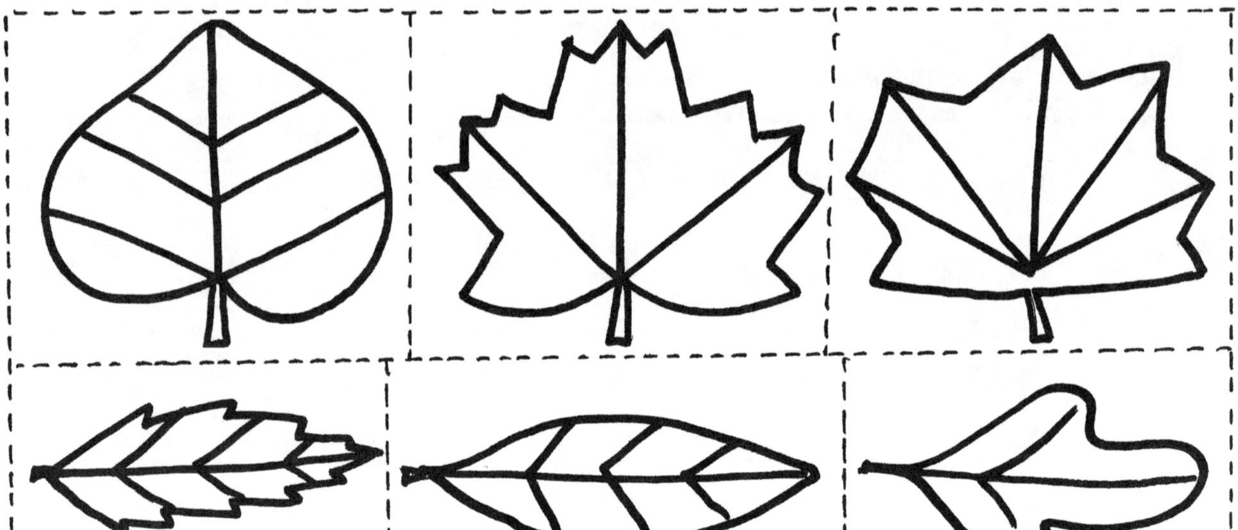

I Like Nuts!

Objectives

✦ Writing and recognizing the following numbers and number words: one, two, three, four, and five.

✦ Identifying different varieties of nuts.

Extension Activities

✦ Collect a variety of nuts and have the children sort the nuts by kind. Give the children a nut graph and have them record how many Brazil nuts, English walnuts, almonds, pecans, and hazelnuts they found.

✦ Make a squirrel out of paper. The squirrel can be made out of a 12" x 9" piece of construction paper.

Cut a 12" x 6" piece of paper for the body, an 8" x 3" piece for the tail, and four 1" x 3" pieces of paper for the legs.

Cut the corners off of the 12" x 6" piece of paper to make the body. The scraps can be used to make the ears.

Cut the corners off of the 8" x 3" piece of paper for the tail. Fringe the tail to make it look bushy.

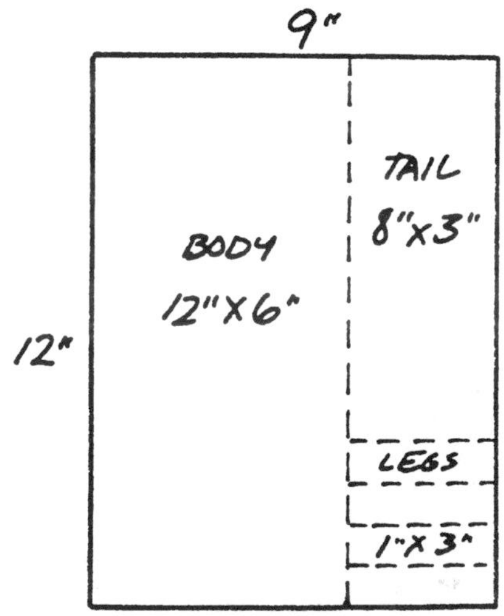

3-D Squirrel Project

Glue the tail and four legs on the body. Add the ears and decorate with crayons or markers.

✦ Use the nuts as a measuring tool and see how many walnuts long the table is. Continue this activity by measuring how many walnuts long your friend, or a piece of paper is.

✦ Give the children a handful of mixed nuts and have them create patterns. An example pattern would be (walnut, walnut, Brazil nut, walnut, walnut, Brazil nut.) If the children are having difficulty making a nut pattern on their own, begin a pattern for them and see if they can continue it.

- ✦ Organize a nut taste test in which the children taste different kinds of nuts. Create a class graph to show which nut the children decide is their favorite.

- ✦ Talk about George Washington Carver, the African American inventor of peanut butter. Sing the song "*Peanut Butter and Jelly.*" Make peanut butter cookies to share with classroom volunteers.

Additional Sources

- ✦ *A Picture Book of George Washington Carver*
  by David Adler & Dan Brown
  (Holiday House, 1999)

- ✦ *Nuts to You*
  by Lois Ehlert
  (Harcourt Brace, 1993)

- ✦ *A Squirrel's Tale*
  by Richard Fowler
  (EDC Publications, 1984)

- ✦ *Peanut Butter and Jelly: A Play Rhyme*
  by Nadine Bernard Westcott
  (EP Dutton, 1992)

- ✦ *Squirrels*
  by Brian Wildsmith
  (Oxford University Press Children's Books, 1984)

I like nuts!

I see ______ Brazil Nut.

I see ___ English Walnuts.

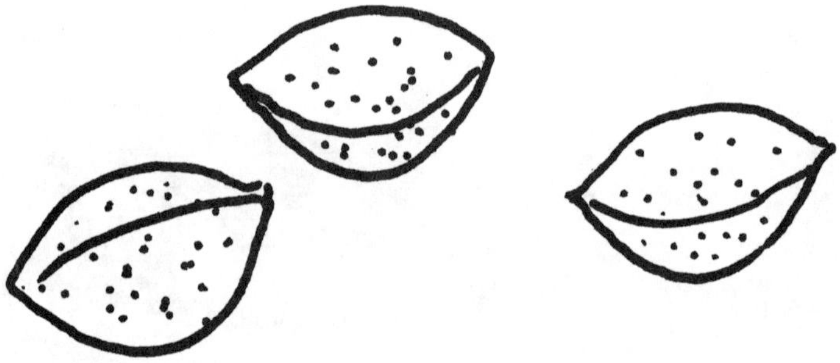

I see ______ almonds.

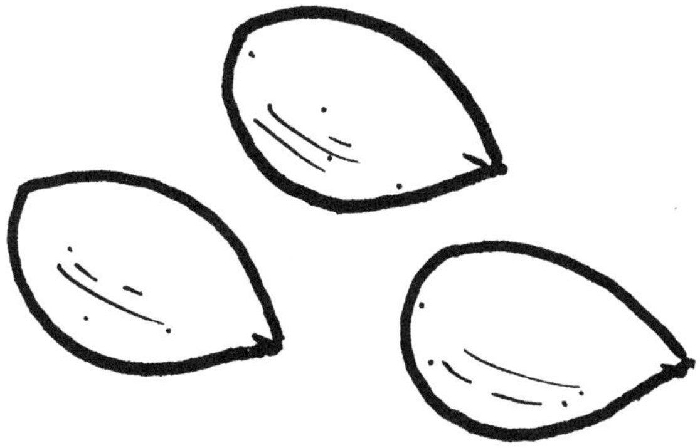

I see ______ pecans.

I see ______ hazelnuts.

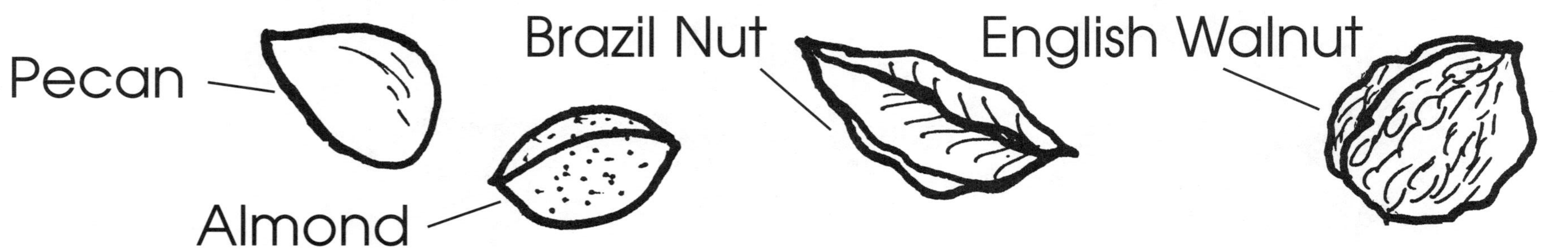

Mixed Nuts

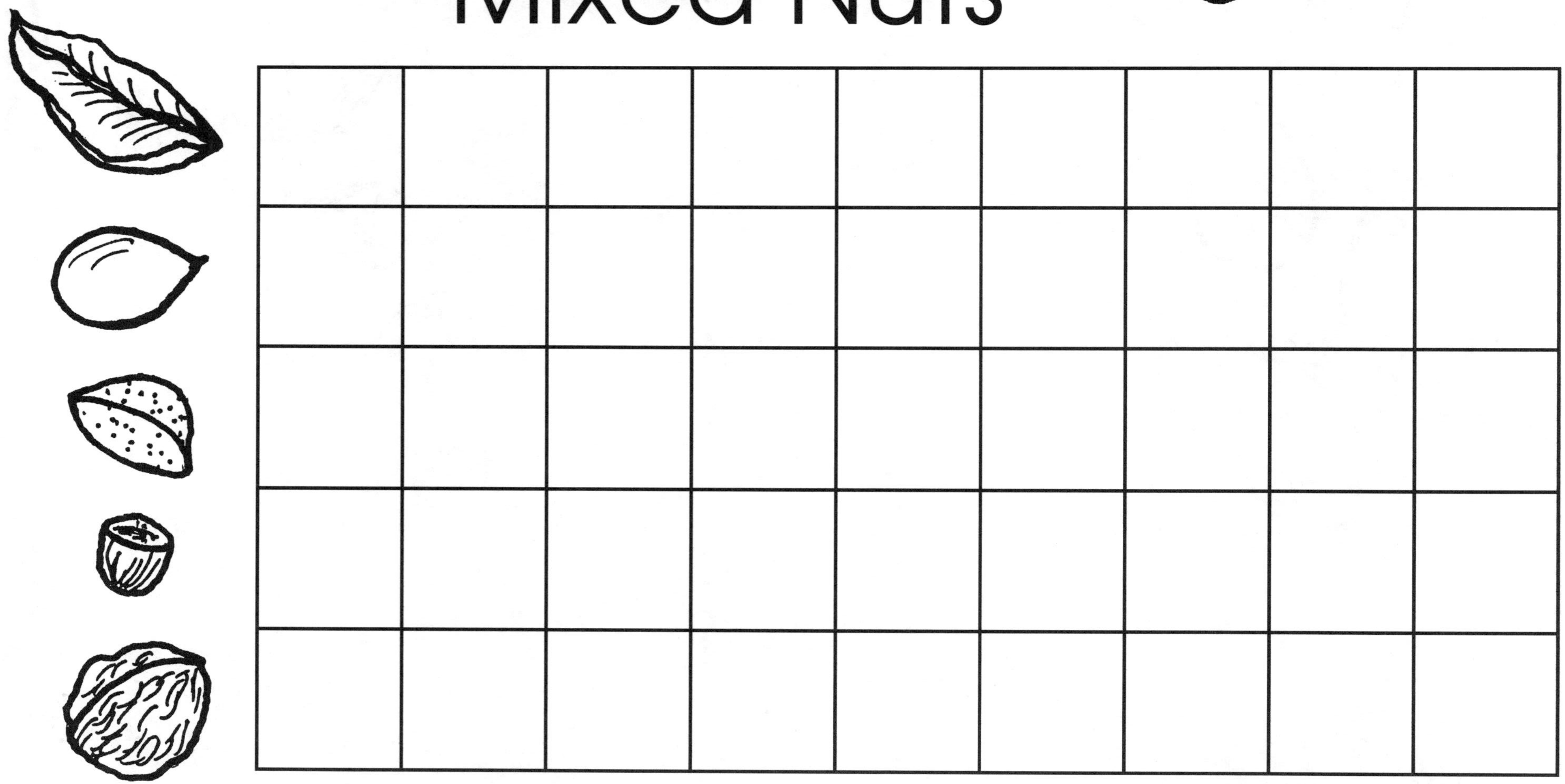

My Fire Book

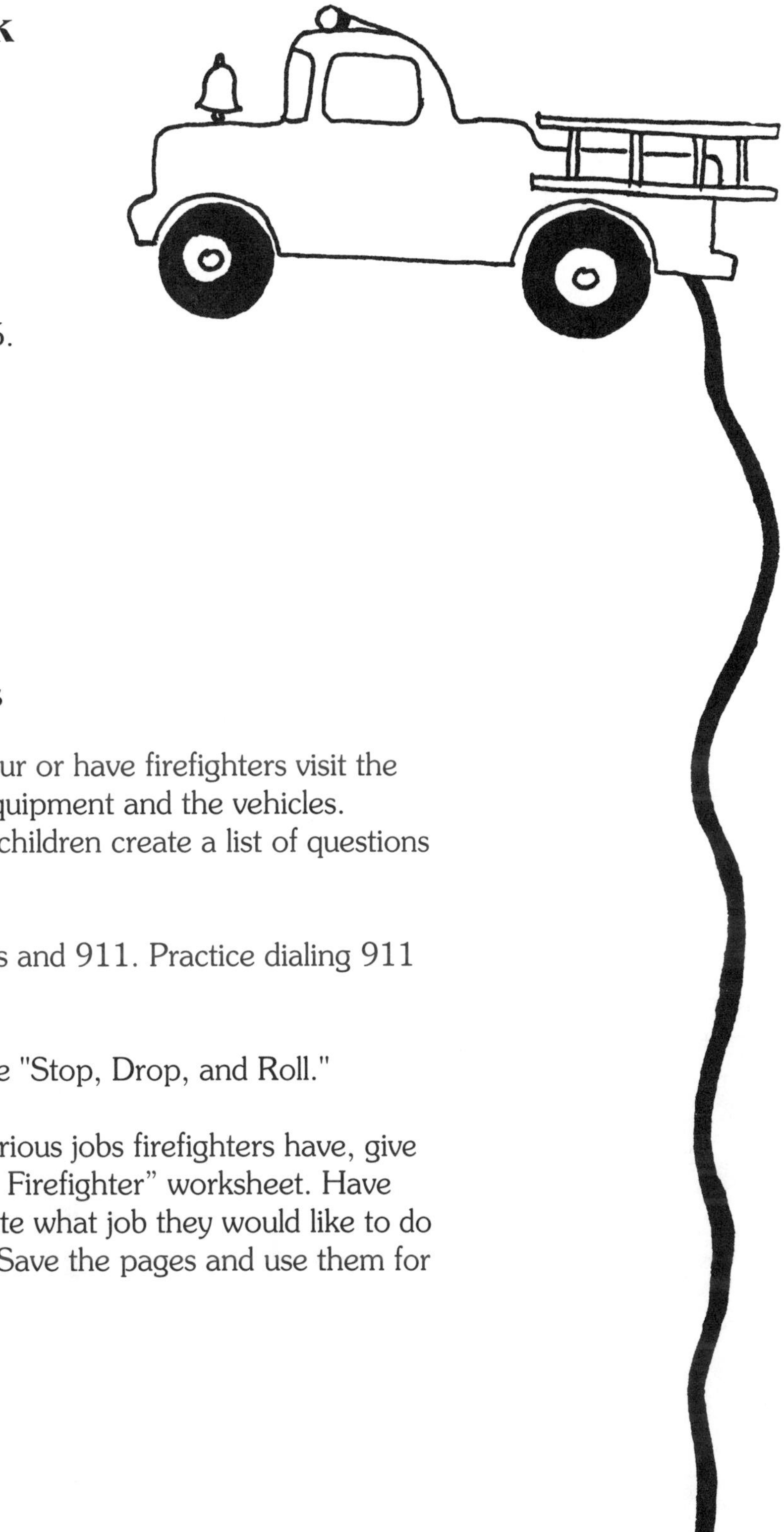

Objectives

- ✦ Counting from 1–5.
- ✦ Recognizing numbers 1–5.
- ✦ Writing numbers 1–5.
- ✦ Reading numbers 1–5.

Extension Activities

- ✦ Visit a fire station for a tour or have firefighters visit the classroom. Look at the equipment and the vehicles. Before the visit, help the children create a list of questions to ask the firefighters.
- ✦ Talk about fire safety rules and 911. Practice dialing 911 on a toy telephone.
- ✦ Have the children practice "Stop, Drop, and Roll."
- ✦ After talking about the various jobs firefighters have, give each child an "If I Were a Firefighter" worksheet. Have the children draw and write what job they would like to do if they were a firefighter. Save the pages and use them for a classroom book.

Additional Sources

- *Fire! Fire! Said Mrs. McGuire*
  by Richard Egielski and Bill Martin Jr.
  (School and Library Binding, 1996)

- *Firehouse Dog*
  by Amy Hutchings
  (Cartwheel Books, 1993)

- *Fighting Fires*
  by Susan Kuklin
  (Aladdin Paperbacks, 1999)

- *The Fire Station*
  by Michael Marchenko and Robert Munsch
  (Annick Press, 1991)

- *Fire Engines*
  by Anne F. Rockwell
  (School and Library Binding, 1986)

My Fire Book

By ______________________________

________ firehouse.

_______ fire engines.

_______ fire coats.

_______ firefighters ready to go.

______ fire hats.

If ______________________ were a firefighter

he or she would _________________________.

The Snowman

Objectives

- ✦ Recognizing the parts of a snowman.
- ✦ Learning basic sight words.
- ✦ Developing confidence as a reader.

Extension Activities

- ✦ Give every child a copy of the "The Snowman" worksheet on page 45 and have them label the parts of the snowman.
- ✦ Create snow people snacks. Give every child some biscuit dough and have them shape the biscuit dough into three balls. Decorate the snow person with raisins, chocolate chips, mini M&M™'s, and Red Hots™. Follow the baking directions on the biscuit container. Cool and eat.
- ✦ Act out the following song:

The Snowman

I am a little snowman.
I am so fat and round.
I started as a snowflake that fell upon the ground.
I have two eyes, a great big scarf of red.
I have a carrot for a nose, a hat upon my head.
Watch me as I melt to the ground!

- ✦ Have an ice cube race. Divide the children into four groups. Group #1 will melt the ice cube with their hands, Group #2 will melt the ice cube by putting it in water, Group #3 will melt the ice cube by putting the ice cube in the air, and Group #4 will melt the ice cube by pouring salt over it. Have the children predict which ice cube will melt first, second, third, and last. Record the results after the race.

- ✦ Create a class book where the children write and draw things they like to do in the snow.

- ✦ Have the children play the "Roll-a-Snowman" game with a partner or have them take the game home for a homework activity. Directions for this game are on page 46.

Additional Sources

- ✦ *Grandpa's Snowman*
  by Gary Barwin
  (Firefly Books, 2000)

- ✦ *The Snowman*
  by Raymond Briggs
  (Random House, 1989)

- ✦ *Snowballs*
  by Lois Ehlert
  (Voyager Picture Books, 1999)

- ✦ *A Snowman Named Just Bob*
  by Mark K. Moulton
  (Lang Graphic Ltd., 1999)

- ✦ *Snowmen at Night*
  by Caralyn Buehner
  (Phyllis Fogelman Books, 2002)

Word List

snow

snowball

hat

carrot

coal

scarf

broom

snowman

sun

By ______________________

The snow

1.

The End

10.

The sun

9.

The snowball

2.

The hat

3.

The snowman

8.

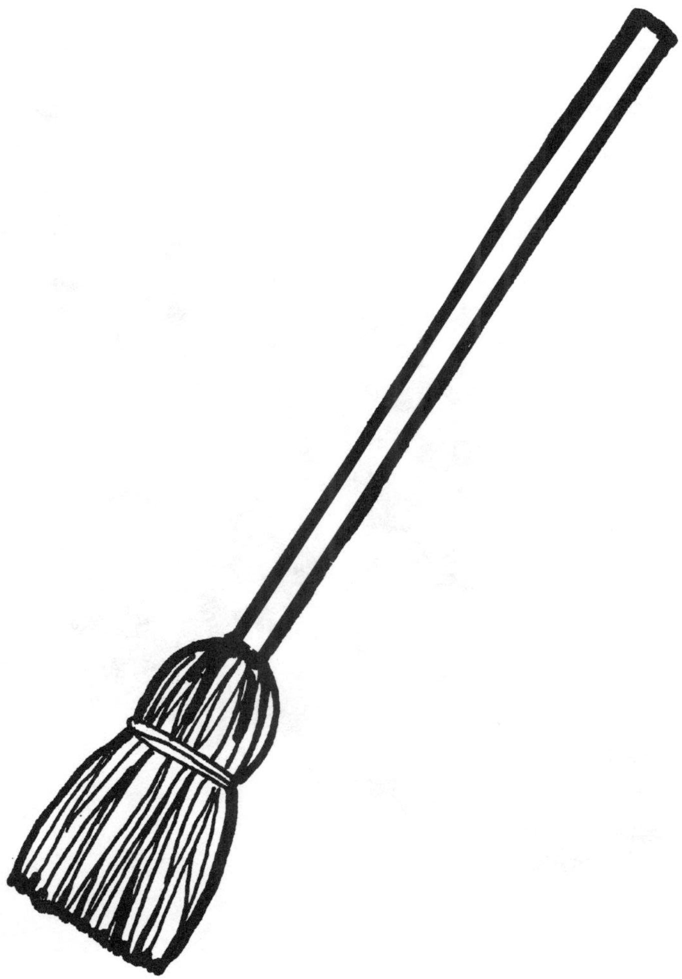

The broom

7.

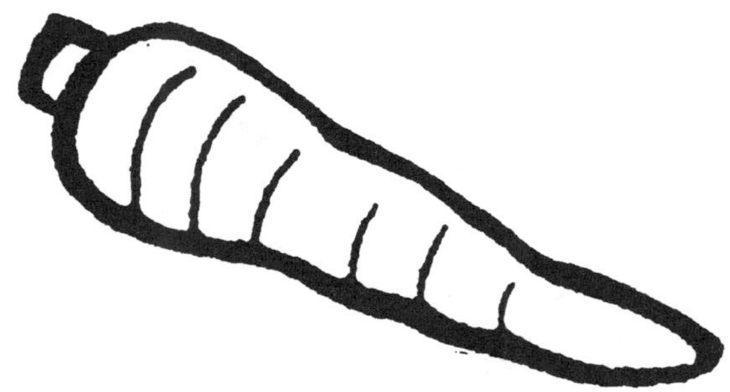

The carrot

4.

The coal

5.

The scarf

6.

Name ______________________________

The Snowman

Roll-a-Snowman

Take turns rolling a die. The first one to finish rolling and drawing a snowman is the winner.

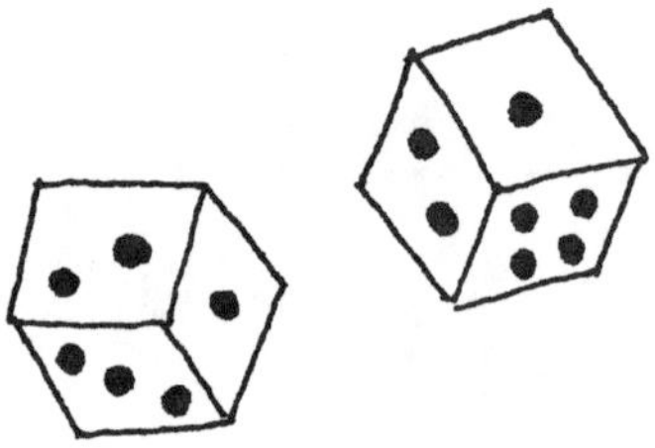

Roll-a-Snowman

 Draw a hat.

 Draw a head.

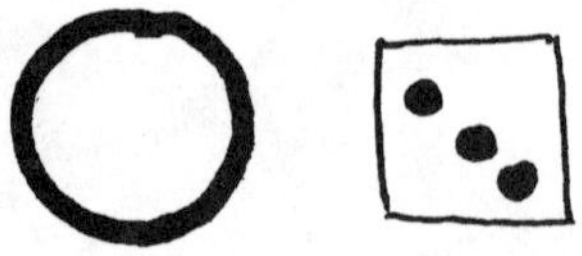 Draw a top body.

 Draw a bottom body.

 Draw a face.

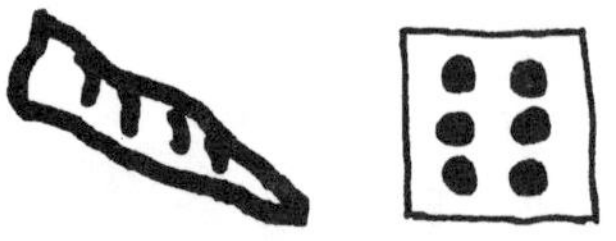 Draw a carrot nose.

Name ____________________

Snowflake Secrets

When it is snowing I like to

____

Snow People Snack

Name ______________________________

- biscuit dough 
- chocolate chips 
- raisins 
- candy 
- Red Hots™ 

1. Wash hands.
2. Shape dough into 3 balls. 
3. Decorate with chocolate chips, raisins, candy, and Red Hots™.
4. Follow baking directions on biscuit package.
5. Eat and enjoy!

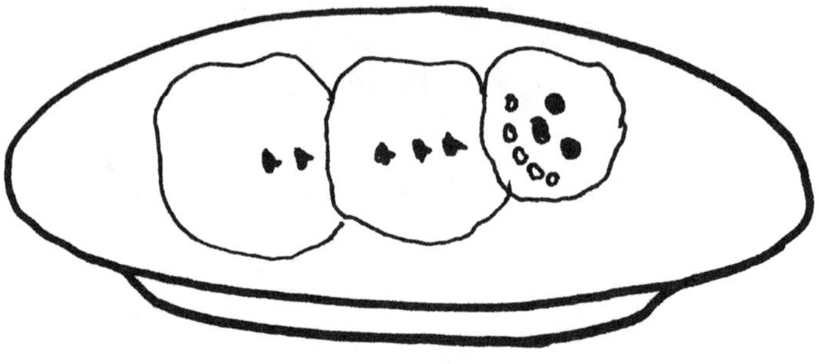

A Rainbow

Objectives

- ✦ Recognizing the following color words: red, orange, yellow, green, blue, and purple.
- ✦ Understanding how a rainbow is formed.
- ✦ Building confidence as a reader.

Extension Activities

- ✦ Explain that a prism reflects light and allows us to see a spectrum. A spectrum shows the colors of the rainbow. Allow the children to explore prisms in the classroom and outside.
- ✦ Allow the children to mix colors. Set up three containers of water mixed with a drop of food coloring. Use the three primary colors (red, yellow, blue.) Give the children eye droppers and have them mix colors in an ice cube tray. Ask them to create the secondary colors (orange, purple and green.)
- ✦ Make a rainbow mobile out of half of a paper plate and tissue paper strips. Cut one inch tissue paper strips of the following colors (red, orange, yellow, green, blue, and purple.) Cut a cloud shape out of half of a paper plate. Glue the color strips in rainbow order to the bottom of the paper plate.
- ✦ Create a class graph where the children decide which color of the rainbow is their favorite.
- ✦ Give every child a rainbow color worksheet from page 55. Have them color the rainbow stripe a color of the rainbow and have them write that color word on the first two lines and on the last line. Have the children draw a picture of something that color in the middle of the rainbow and write the word on the third line. Example: Red, red, a strawberry is red.

Additional Sources

- *Lightning and Rainbows*
  by Michael Carroll
  (Chariot Victor Publishing, 1997)

- *Why We Have Rainbows*
  by Linda Finely-Day & Liz McIntosh
  (Broadman and Holman Publishers, 1998)

- *Swinging on a Rainbow*
  by Thomas Hamilton & Charles Perking
  (Africa World Press Inc., 1993)

A Rainbow

By ______________________

2.

Some ______________________

1.

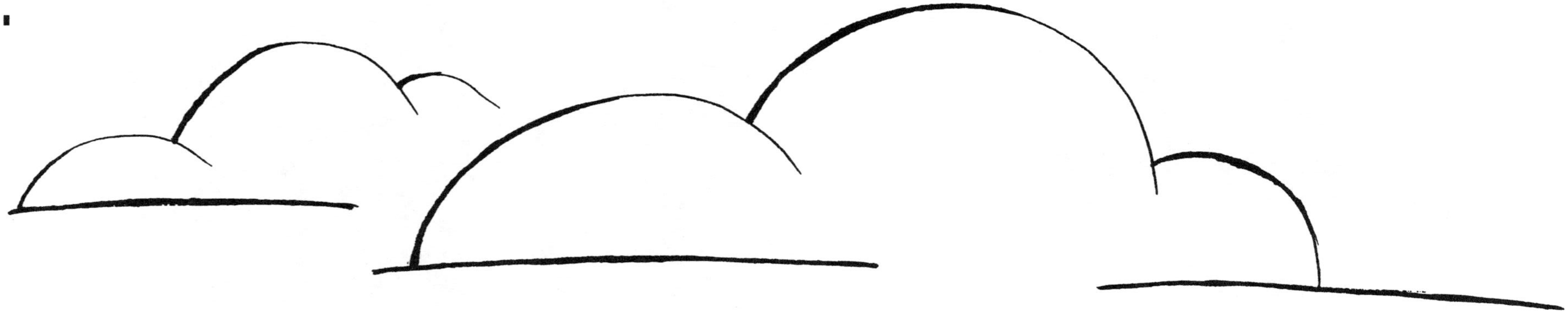

Some ________________

3.

The ________________

4.

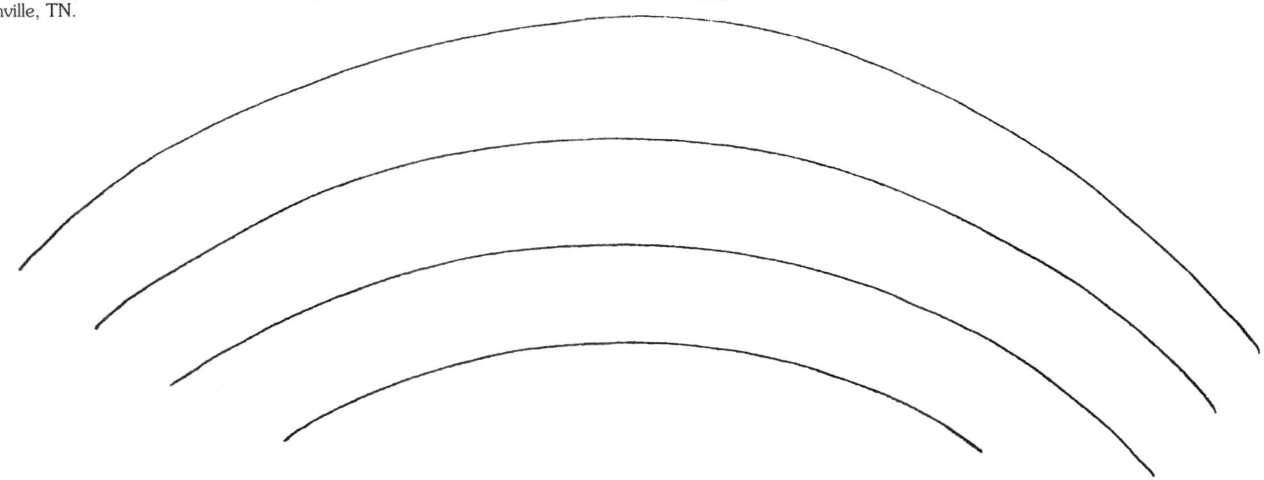

See ______________, ______________, and ______________.

6.

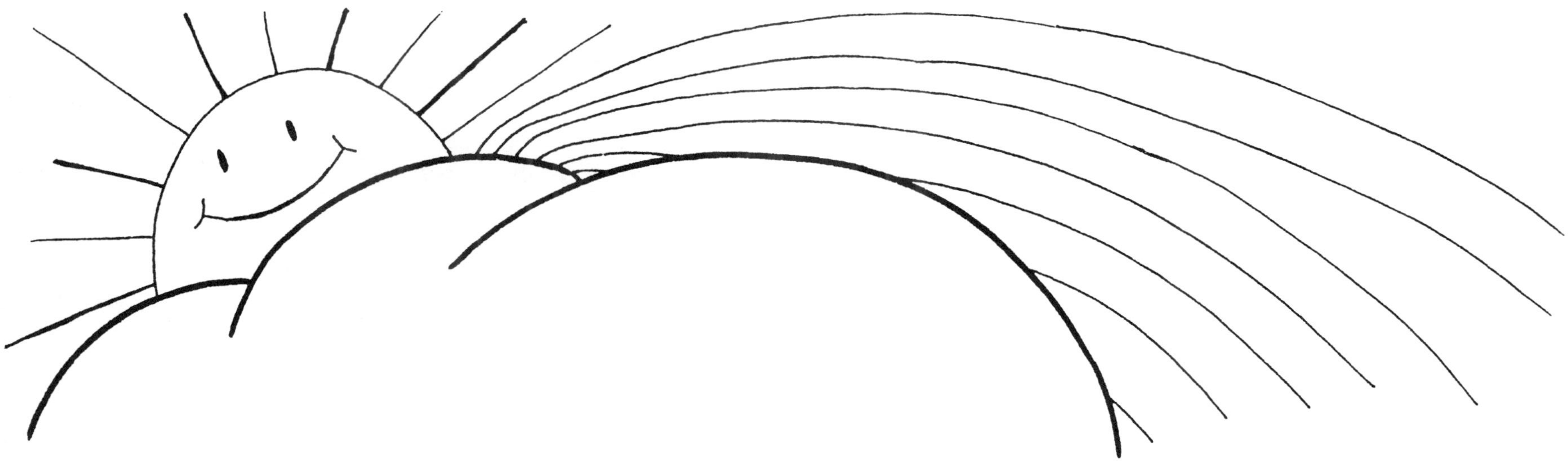

A ______________________________

5.

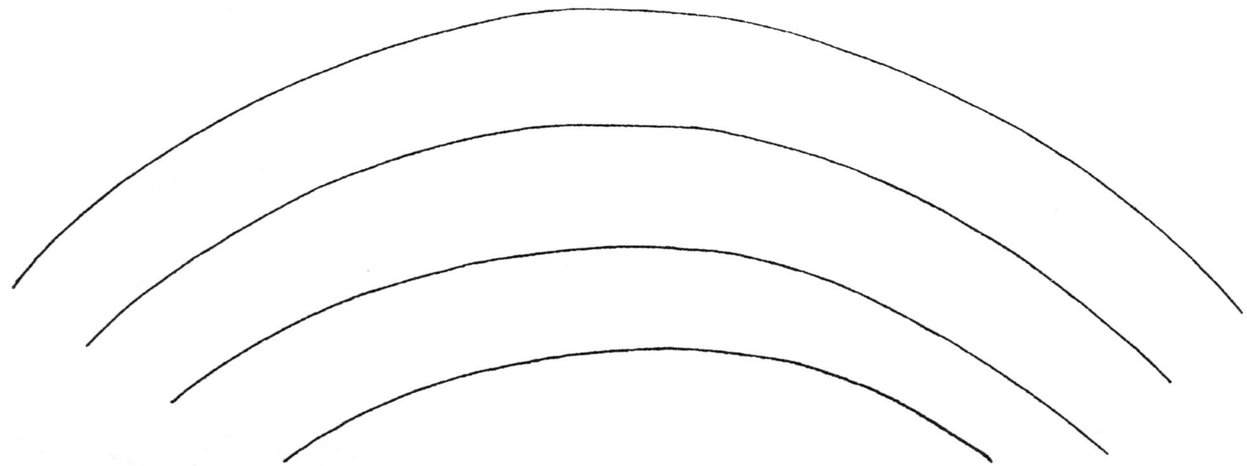

See __________, __________, and __________.

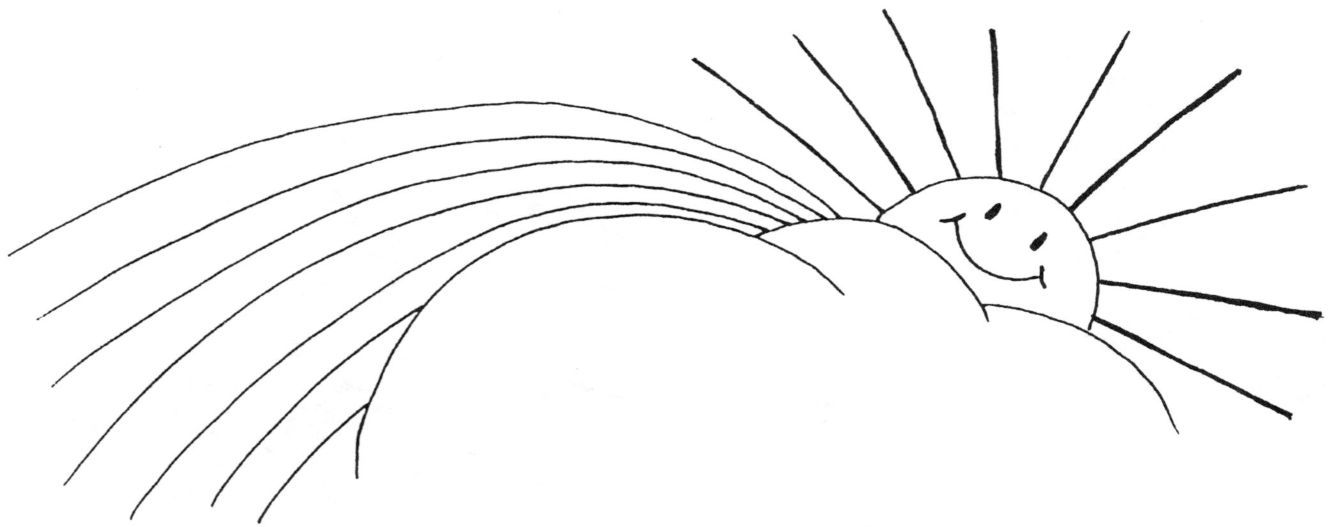

Happy Day!

Rainbow Color Worksheet

Name ______________________

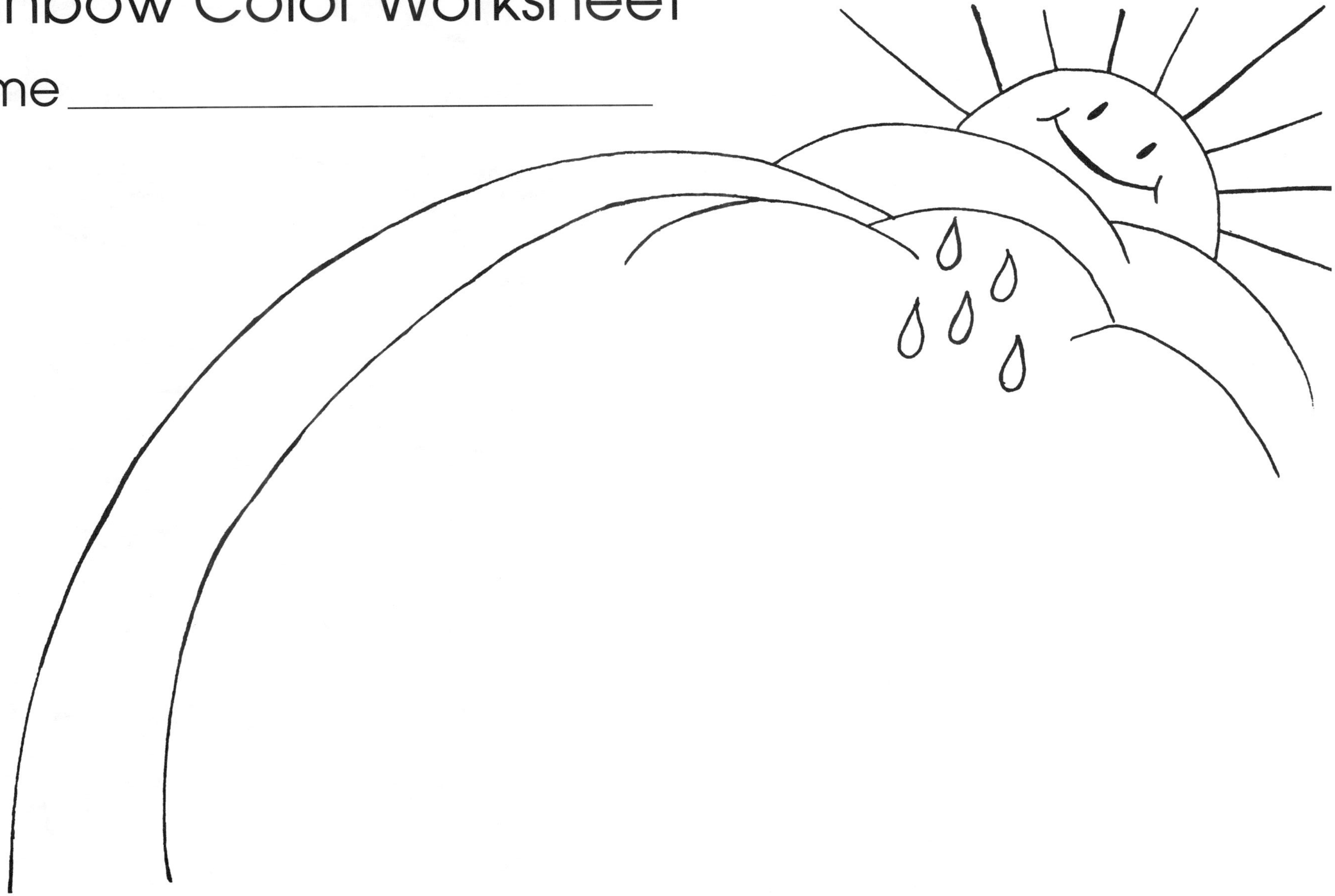

__________, __________, a __________ is __________.

Color Mixing

Name ____________________

Jack - O - Faces

Objectives

- ✦ Recognizing different emotions and facial expressions.
- ✦ Building confidence as a reader.

Extension Activities

- ✦ Teach the children the following poem.

Five Little Pumpkins

Five little pumpkins sitting on a gate.
The first one said, "Oh my, it's getting late."
The second one said, "There are witches in the air."
The third one said, "But we don't care."
The fourth one said, "Let's run, and run, and run."
The fifth one said, "I'm ready for some fun!"
Oooo went the wind, and out went the lights
and the five little pumpkins rolled out of sight.

- ✦ Give every student a copy of the pumpkins and gate worksheets on pages 63 and 64. Have them color and cut out the pumpkins. Use the worksheet to act out the "Five Little Pumpkins" poem on page 63 or read one of the Five Little Pumpkin books.

- ✦ Use the pumpkins and gate worksheets on pages 63 and 64 to act out math story problems.

  Example: There are five little pumpkins sitting on a gate.
  Two roll away.
  How many pumpkins are left sitting on the gate?

- ✦ Carve a classroom jack-o-lantern. Before carving the pumpkin, create a class graph where the children choose what kind of eyes, nose, and mouth they want the jack-o-lantern to have:

eyes — ●●, ■■, ▲▲, ▼▼, ◆◆

nose — ●, ■, ▲, ▼, ◆

mouth — 

Additional Sources

- *Pumpkin Soup*
  by Helen Cooper
  (Farrar Straus & Giroux, 1999)

- *Pumpkin Day, Pumpkin Night*
  by Anne F. Rockwell
  (Walker & Company Library, 1999)

- *Five Little Pumpkins*
  by Iris Van Rynbach
  (Boyds Mills Press, 1995)

- *Five Little Pumpkins*
  by Dan Yaccarino
  (Harpercollins Juvenile Books, 1998)

By ______________________________

2.

This is Jack-O-Sad.

1.

This is Jack-O-Happy.

3.

Now you see him sleepy.

4.

Now you see him mad.

6.

But in a pie he's best of all!

5.

This is Jack in pieces small.

Five Little Pumpkins

Color and cut out the five pumpkins.

Use the pumpkins to act out the song "Five Little Pumpkins."

5 Little Pumpkins

Five Little Pumpkins

Five little pumpkins sitting on a gate.
The first one said,
"Oh my, it's getting late."
The second one said,
"There are witches in the air."
The third one said,
"But we don't care."
The fourth one said,
"Let's run, and run, and run."
The fifth one said,
"I'm ready for some fun!"
Oooo went the wind,
and out went the lights
and the five little pumpkins
rolled out of sight.

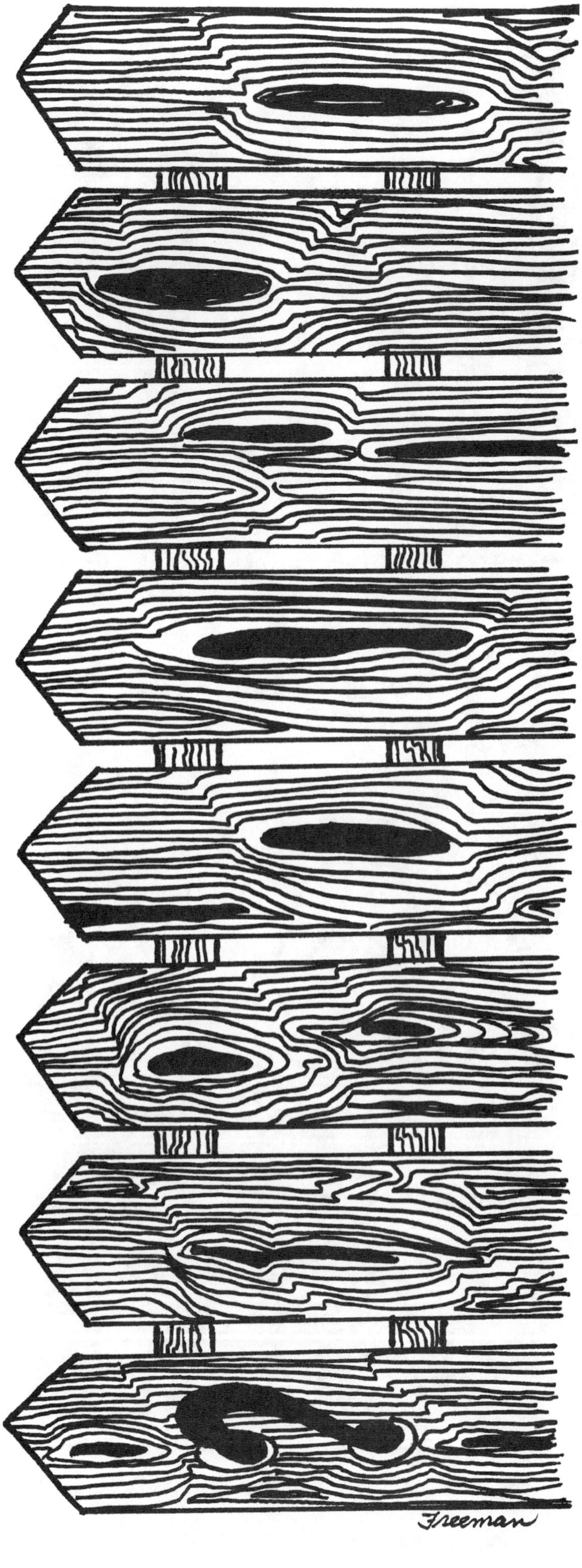
Freeman

Turkeys on Parade

Objectives

- ✦ Recognizing the color words in context: brown, red, and orange.
- ✦ Building confidence as a reader.

Extension Activities

- ✦ Create a class book in which the children can draw and write about things for which they are thankful.See page 71 for a template.

- ✦ Send the "Decorate a Turkey" family project on page 70 home with each child. Have the child and his/her family work together to decorate the turkey. Encourage them to be creative. Some examples of materials to use are: cotton balls, glitter, markers, stickers, cereal, spices, feathers, wallpaper, paint. Have the children bring their turkeys back to school and create a display to share with others.

- ✦ Have the children play the "Healthy/Not Healthy" nutrition game. Create the game by cutting pictures of healthy and unhealthy foods out of grocery ads and magazines. Glue the food pictures onto paper or tagboard to create cards.

  Draw a smiley face on the back of all of the healthy food cards and a sad face on the back of the unhealthy food cards. Get two paper plates and write the word "healthy" on one plate and the phrase "not healthy" on the other plate. Have the children sort the food cards by placing all of the cards with healthy foods on the "healthy" paper plate and all of the unhealthy foods on the "not healthy" paper plate.

  Have the children check their answers by turning each food card over. If the food is healthy it will have a smiley face on the back; if the food is unhealthy it will have a sad face on the back.

Additional Sources

- *A Turkey for Thanksgiving*
  by Eve Bunting
  (Clarion Books, 1995)

- *The Turkey Saves the Day*
  by Shelagh Canning
  (Troll Association, 1997)

- *Gracias, The Thanksgiving Turkey*
  by Joy Cowley
  (Scholastic Trade, 1998)

- *Thanksgiving Day*
  by Gail Gibbons
  (Cartwheel Books, 1999)

- *Twas the Night Before Thanksgiving*
  by Dave Pilkey
  (Orchard Books, 1990)

Turkeys on Parade

By ______________________________

Here comes the brown turkey
gobble, gobble, gobble.

Here comes the red turkey
ruffle, ruffle, ruffle.

Here comes the orange turkey
fluff, fluff, fluffle.

Here come all the turkeys
strut, strut, wobble.

Here comes the turkey.
Mmmm . . . Mmmm . . . Mmmmm
Happy Thanksgiving!

Decorate A Turkey

______________________ is thankful for

____.

Turkey Math

Name ____________________

Roll the die.

Write the number on the turkey's body.

Draw that many feathers on the turkey.

My Christmas Tree Book

Objectives

- ✦ Recognizing the numbers in context: one, two, three, four, and five.
- ✦ Recognizing the shapes: star, square, heart, triangle, and circle.
- ✦ Building confidence as a reader.

Extension Activities

✦ Give each child a copy of the blank Christmas tree worksheet on page 79. Have the children decorate the Christmas tree by drawing the following shapes on the tree: star, square, heart, triangle, and circle. Have the children draw the shapes until the tree is completely filled.

After the tree is decorated, give each child a copy of the Christmas Tree Math worksheet on page 81. Have the children look at their decorated tree and complete the graph by coloring in one square for each shape that they drew. Or have them exchange their tree with a friend and complete the graph using their friend's tree.

If you don't want the children to decorate their own tree, give them the Christmas tree worksheet on page 80 that is already decorated and have them complete the graph using that tree.

✦ Make ornaments for the birds out of pine cones, peanut butter, and birdseed. Spread peanut butter over a pine cone and then roll the pine cone in birdseed. Attach a piece of yarn to the top of the pine cone so the pine cone can be hung on a tree for the birds to eat.

Additional Sources

- *A Possible Tree*
  by Josephine Haskell Aldridge
  (Aladdin Paperbacks, 1998)

- *Christmas Tree Memories*
  by Aliki
  (Harper Trophy, 1994)

- *Chita's Christmas Tree*
  by Fitzgerald Howard
  (Aladdin Books, 1993)

- *My Wonderful Christmas Tree*
  by Dahlov Zorach Ipcar
  (Down East Books, 1999)

- *O Christmas Tree*
  by Vashanti Rahaman
  (Boyds Mills Press, 1996)

- *The After-Christmas Tree*
  by Linda Wagner Tyler
  (Puffin, 1992)

Two ☐ ornaments

Three ♡ ornaments

One ☆ ornament

Four ○ ornaments

Merry Christmas!

Match the word to the number.

one	3
two	1
three	5
four	2
five	4

Merry Christmas

Five △ ornaments

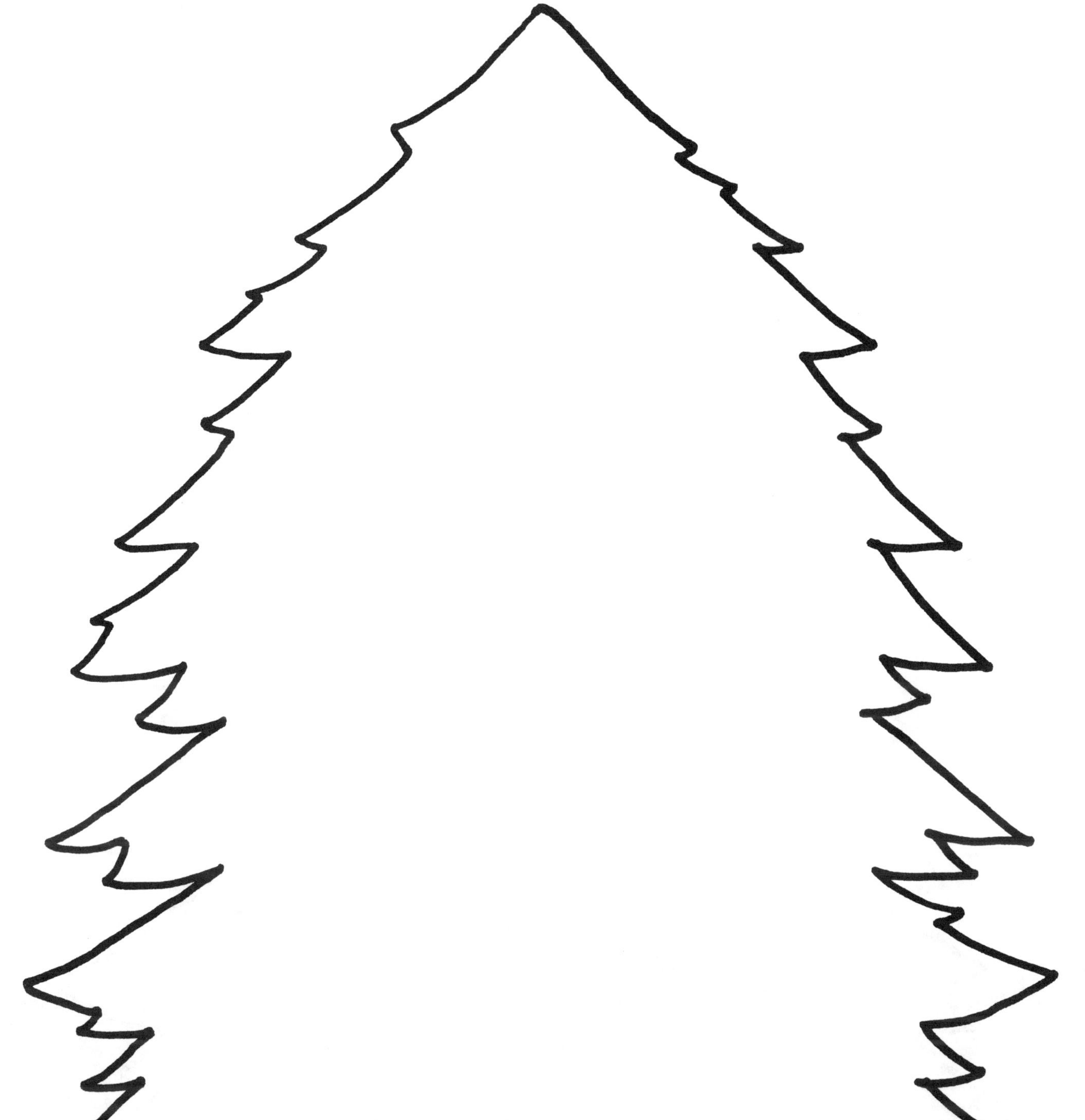

Name ____

Name ______________________________

Christmas Tree Math

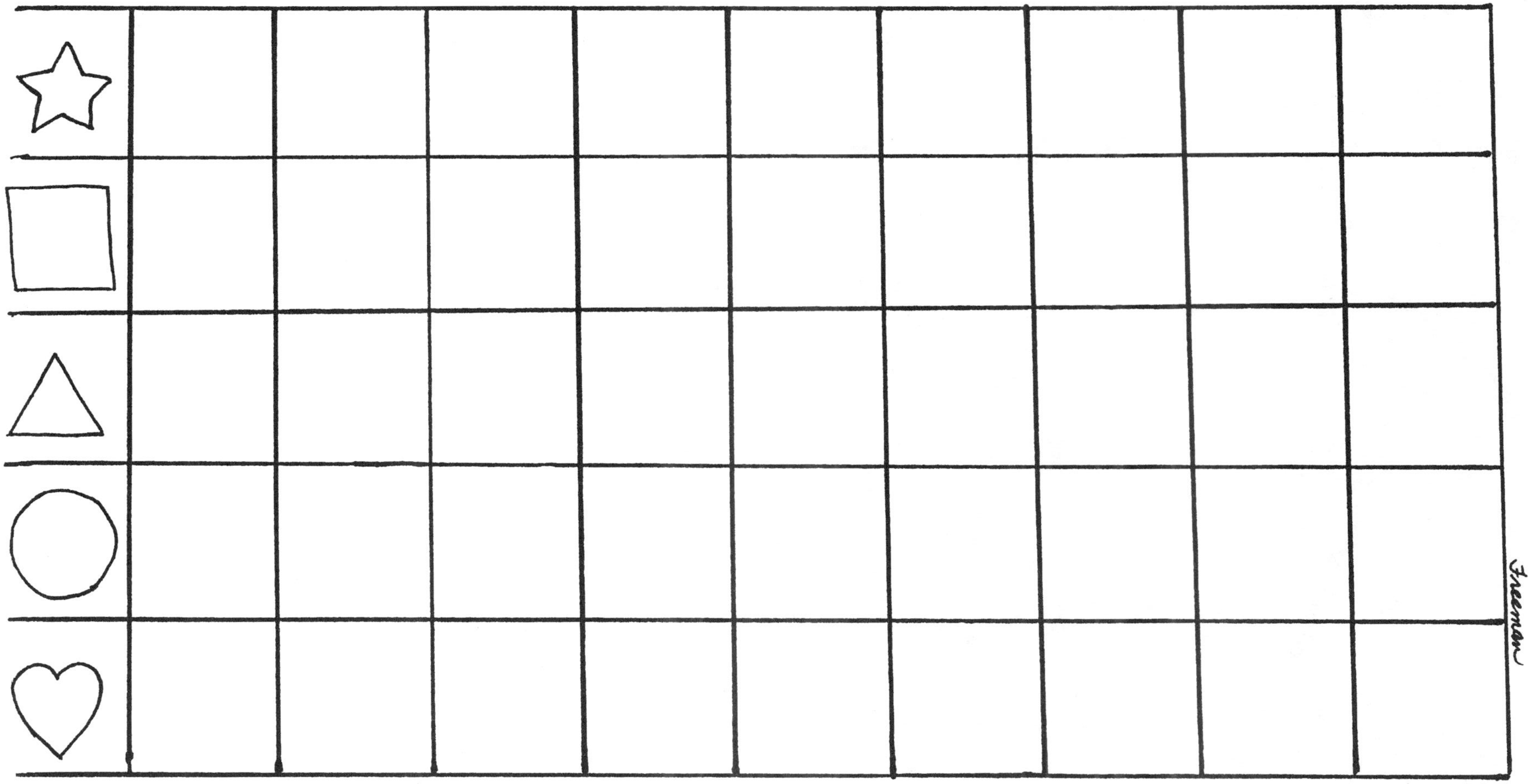

Name ______________________________

Holiday Family Project

Decorate this ornament with your family.

A Cat

Objectives

- ✦ Identifying the parts of a cat in context: head, whiskers, nose, tail.
- ✦ Building confidence as a reader.

Extension Activities

- ✦ Create a class graph showing what kind of animal the children would like as a pet.
- ✦ Make a cat out of construction paper.

---

1. 1 – Body 9" x 12" 

---

2. 2 – 6" x 6"

(1) Head cut

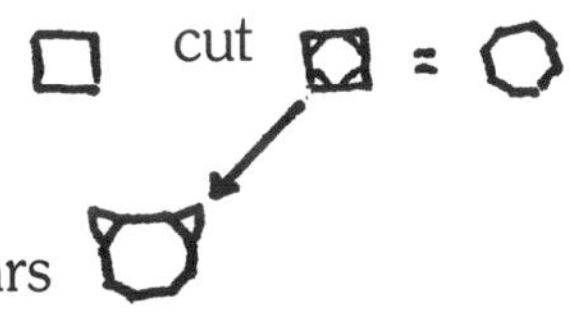

(2) Tail

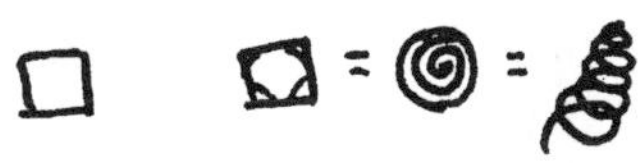

3. Whiskers $3\frac{1}{16}$" x 12"
   cut on paper cutter

   pink – △ for the nose 1" x 1" use one

   red – △ for the mouth 1" x 1" use one

1- 3" x 3" colored paper for bow cut

1- 1" x 1" colored paper for eyes cut

✦ Conduct the following science experiment to answer the question: Do cats always land on their feet?

Give each child a cat worksheet. Have the children color and cut out the cat pattern and fold it along the dashed lines. Then cut out the head and glue the head to the body.

When the glue is dry, hold the cat upside down by the belly and drop it to the floor.

Before the children test their paper cats, have them predict what they think will happen. Does the cat flip over and land on its feet? How close to the floor can you hold your cat and still give it time to flip over?

Remind the children never to toss or drop a real cat.

Additional Sources

✦ *Cats*
by Gail Gibbons
(Holiday House, 1998)

✦ *Black Cat*
by Christopher Myers
(Scholastic Trade, 1999)

✦ *Duncan and Delores*
by Barbara Samuels
(Bradbury Press, 1986)

✦ *Cats and Kittens*
by Katherine Starke
(Educational Development Center, 1998)

A Cat

By ______________________________

A cat has ______________________.

1.

A cat has a ____________________.

3.

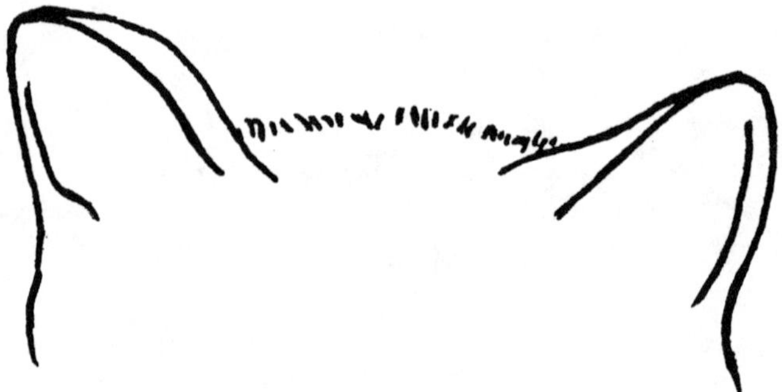

A cat has ____________________.

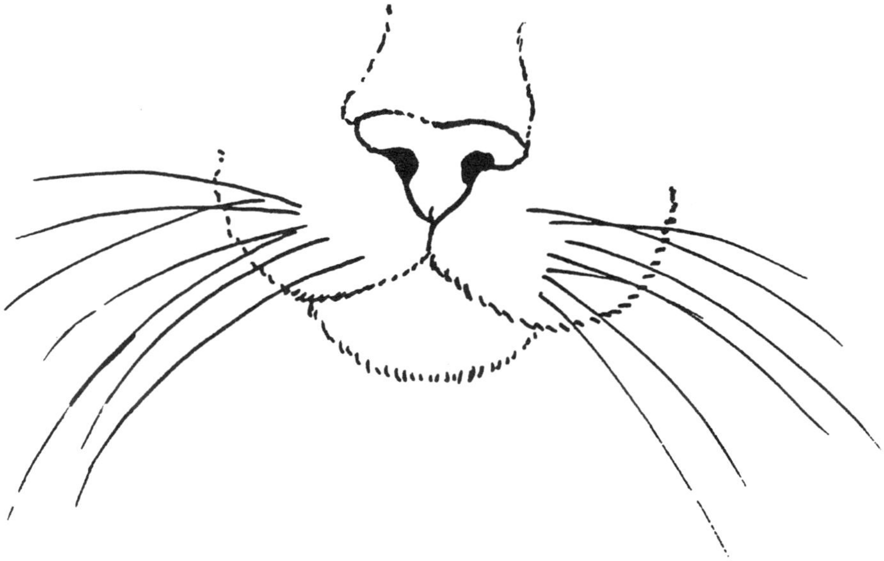

4.

A cat has ______________.

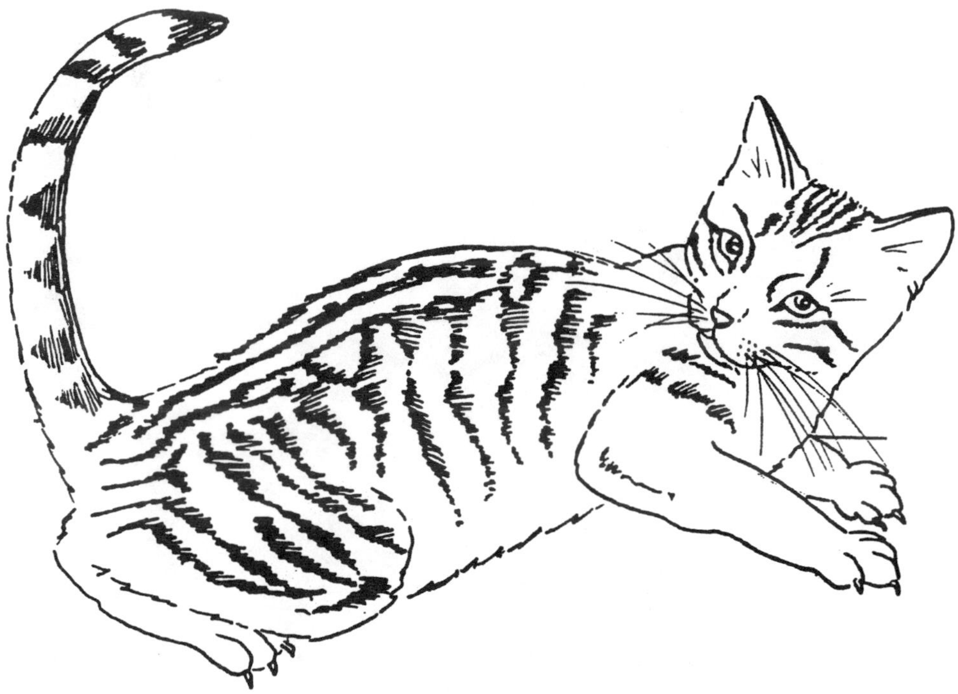

6.

Purr, ______________.

5.

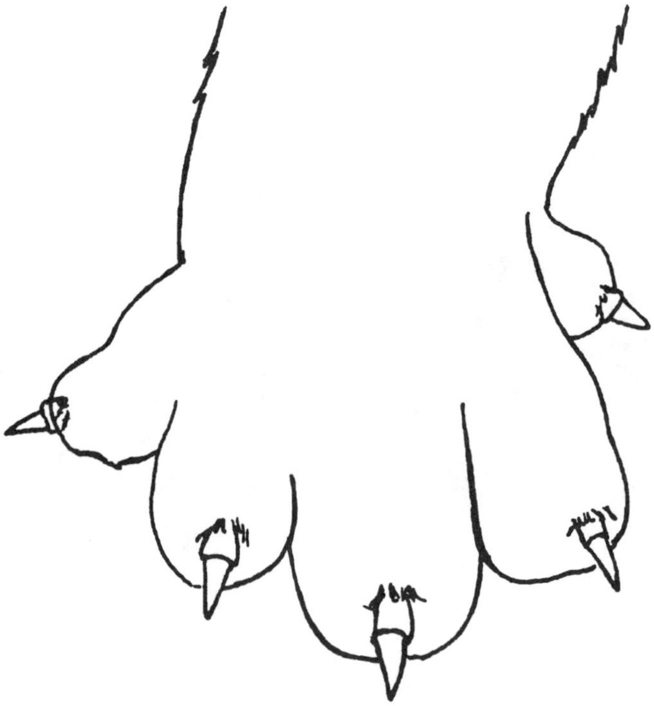

A cat has ______________.

The End

My Cat

Name ______________________________

My cat has a ______________________ .

My cat has ______________________ .

My cat has a ______________________ .

My cat's tail is ______________  long.

My cat's tail is ______________  long.

My cat has ______________ .

My cat's name is ______________________.

Cat Worksheet

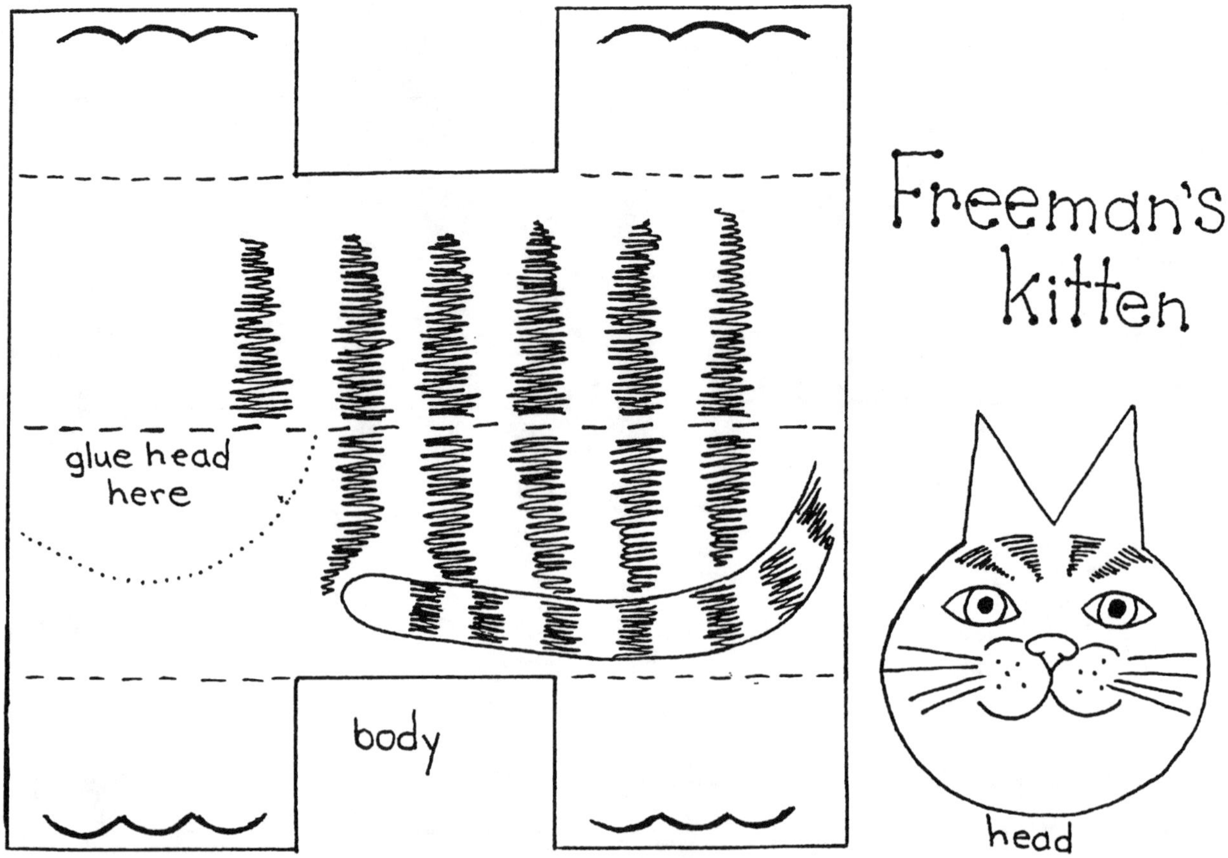

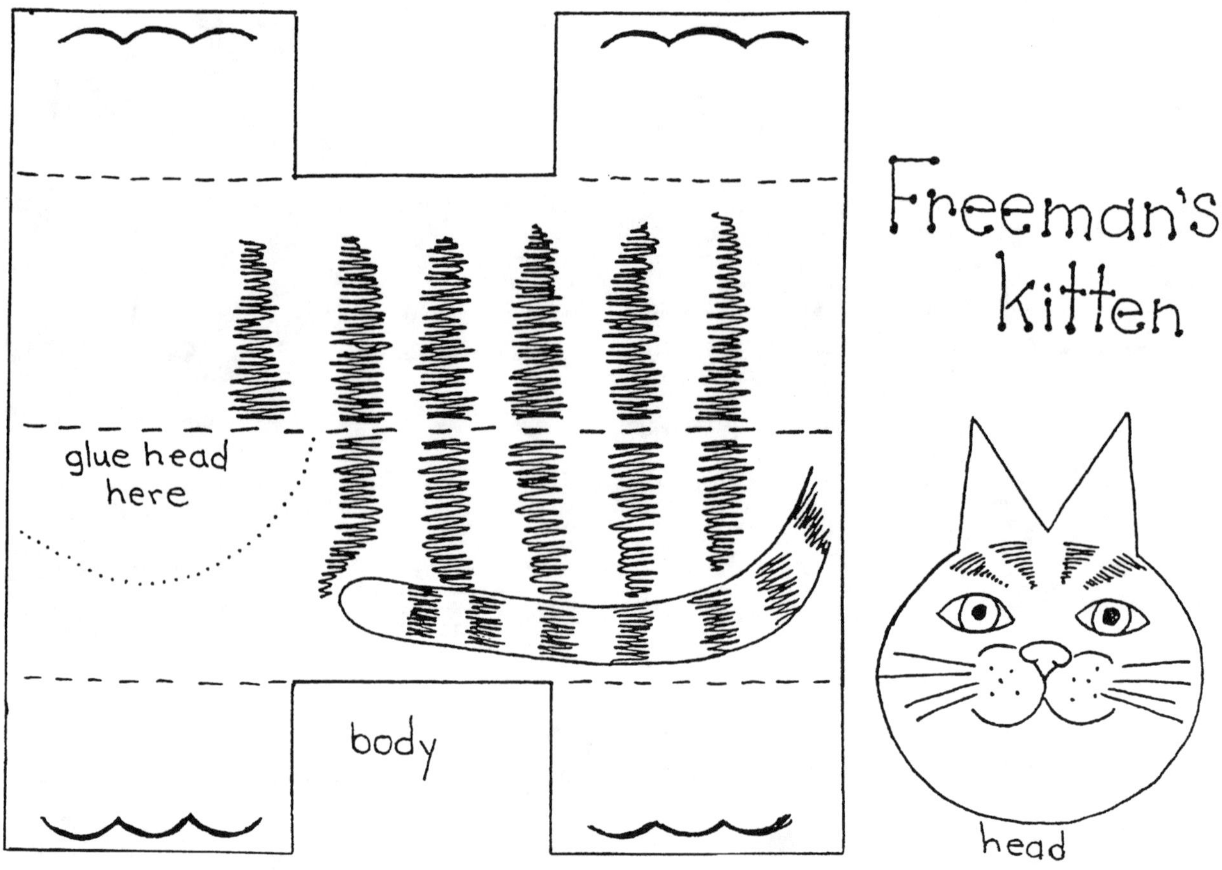

Cat Rap

Objectives

- ✦ Introducing students to the breeds of cats in context: Tabby, Tortoiseshell, Siamese, Manx, Persian, Calico, and Russian Blue.
- ✦ Building confidence as a reader.

Extension Activities

- ✦ Create a class graph showing which breed of cat each child decides is his or her favorite. Glue a picture of the following cats on a large piece of paper: Tabby, Tortoiseshell, Siamese, Manx, Persian, Calico, Russian Blue. Create a column for each type of cat. Have the children choose which breed of cat is their favorite. Have them glue a picture of that cat on the graph under their favorite breed.
- ✦ Give the children a copy of the "My Favorite Cat" graph on page 98 and have them ask their friends which breed of cat is their favorite. Have the children record the results on their graph. Have the children share their results with the class.
- ✦ Fill the play area with the following items: cat stuffed animals, litter boxes, cat bowls, collars, cat care books, cat posters, cat food, cat beds, and cat toys. Give the children time to explore the cat items and interact with each other.
- ✦ Make a cat mask out of a paper plate and decorate it with markers, construction paper, and crayons. Help the children cut holes in their paper plates for the eyes, nose, and mouth. Have the children wear their masks and get on the floor and walk like a cat. Ask the children to act like a cat by stretching, rolling, and meowing.

- ✦ Give every child a cat stuffed animal and have them practice proper cat safety. Have the children practice petting a cat by moving their hands gently over the cat's back in the direction the cat's fur grows.

Additional Sources

- *ABC Cats*
  by Kathy Darling
  (Walker & Company, 1998)

- *Top Cat*
  by Lois Ehlert
  (Harcourt Brace, 1998)

- *Calico's Cousins*
  by Phyllis Limbacher Tildes
  (Charlesbridge Publishing, 1999)

- *Ginger*
  by Charlotte Voake
  (Candlewick Press, 2000)

Cat Rap

By ______________________________

5.

Persian, Calico,

1.

Tabby, Tortoiseshell,

4.

I give thanks.

2.

Siamese, Manx.

6.

Russian Blue.

3.

For all these little creatures,

7.

Every type of kitty cat,

8.

The End

My Favorite Cat

By ____________.

10.							
9.							
8.							
7.							
6.							
5.							
4.							
3.							
2.							
1.							
	Tabby	Tortoiseshell	Persian	Calico	Russian Blue	Siamese	Manx

The Spider

Objectives

✦ Building confidence as a reader.

✦ Being exposed to basic sight words.

Extension Activities

✦ Create and provide each child with a picture of a spider and have them label the parts of a spider: eight legs, eyes, and two body parts.

✦ Create a Venn diagram where the children identify how spiders and insects are alike and how spiders and insects are different such as: spiders have 8 legs and insects have 6 legs; spiders have two body parts and insects have three body parts; insects have antennae and spiders do not.

✦ Give every child a plastic spider ring and have them use the ring to act out Raffi's song *Spider on the Floor* by Bill Russell.

✦ Make a spider web by putting a piece of black construction paper in a box and rolling a marble in white paint. Place the paint coated marble on the black paper and move the box back and forth. This will create a marble painting that looks like a spider web. Have the children draw a spider on white paper, cut out the drawing, and glue it onto the web.

✦ Give every child a spider snack recipe on page 104 and help the children make the snack.

✦ Sing and act out the song "Itsy Bitsy Spider." Sing the song using "itsy bitsy" the first time through and sing using a middle voice and regular hand motions. Then sing the song replacing "itsy bitsy" with "big fat." Sing with a low voice and make big motions. Finally sing the song replacing "big fat" with "teeny weeny." Sing with a high voice and make small motions.

Additional Sources

- *The Very Busy Spider*
  by Eric Carle
  (Putnam Publishing Group, 1989)

- *Spiders*
  by Gail Gibbons
  (Holiday House, 1994)

- *The Lady and the Spider*
  by Faith McNulty
  (Harper Trophy, 1987)

- *Spider on the Floor (Raffi Songs to Read)*
  by Bill Russell
  (Crown Publishing, 1996)

- *The Itsy Bitsy Spider*
  by Iza Trapani
  (Whispering Coyote Press, 1997)

The Spider

by ____________________

2.

The web.

1.

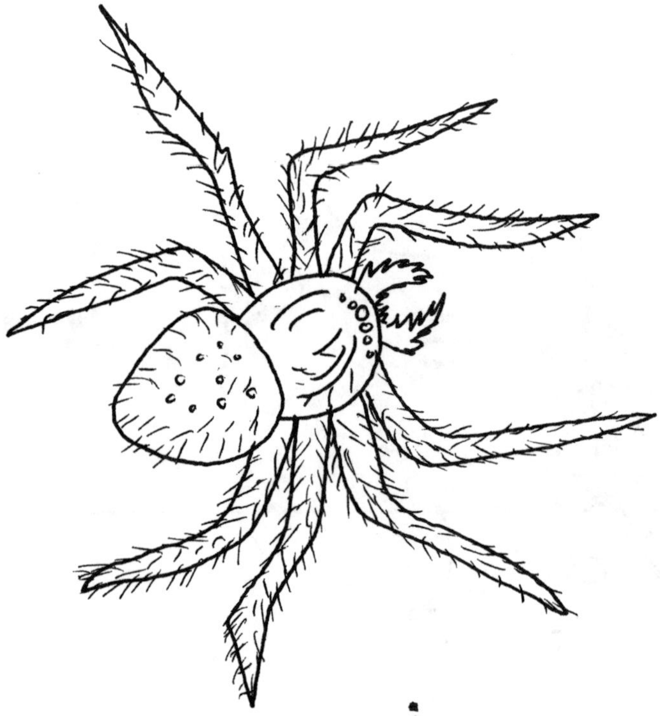

The spider.

3.

The fly.

4.

Mmm . . . . lunch!

5.

The spider. The web. Where is the fly?

Spider Snack

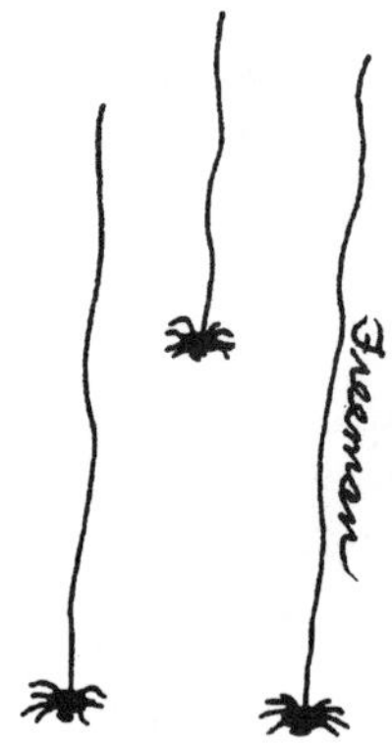

- 2 round crackers 
- 8 pretzel sticks 
- 2 raisins 
- peanut butter 

1. Spread peanut butter on crackers.

2. Add 2 raisins  for eyes.

3. Add 8 pretzels  for legs.

4. Eat and enjoy. 

A Wind Quintet

Objectives

✦ Recognizing the instruments in a wind quintet: flute, oboe, clarinet, bassoon, and French horn.

✦ Identifying that *quintet* means "a group of five."

✦ Determining which instrument in a woodwind quintet you would like to play.

Extension Activities

✦ Make a class graph to be used to help the children decide which instrument in a wind quintet they would like to play.

✦ Make a shaker by folding a paper plate in half and filling it with one of the following: rice, rocks, or beans. Staple the sides together, then decorate the outside of the paper plate with crayons, markers, stickers, paint, or streamers. Take turns listening to the shakers and determining what is inside. Finally, practice keeping the beat to a song by shaking the shaker.

✦ Talk about the four instrument families: strings, brass, woodwinds, and percussion. Compare how the instruments are the same and how they are different. What families do the wind quintet instruments fit into?

✦ After seeing and hearing different kinds of instruments, make a class book in which each child draws a picture of his/her favorite instrument.

✦ Listen to the following recordings featuring the instruments in a woodwind quintet: *Peter and the Wolf* by Prokofiev
Bolero by Ravel
A Young Person's Guide to the Orchestra by Britten.

Additional Sources

- *Classical Cats: A Children's Introduction to the Orchestra*
  by David Chesky
  (Chesky Records, 1997)

- *Meet the Orchestra*
  by Ann Hayes and Karen Thompson
  (Harcourt Brace, 1995)

- *Musical Instruments from A to Z*
  by Bobbie Kalman
  (Crabtree Publishing, 1997)

- *Zin! Zin! Zin! A Violin*
  by Lloyd Moss and Marjorie Priceman
  (Aladdin Paperbacks, 2000)

A Wind Quintet

By ____________________________________

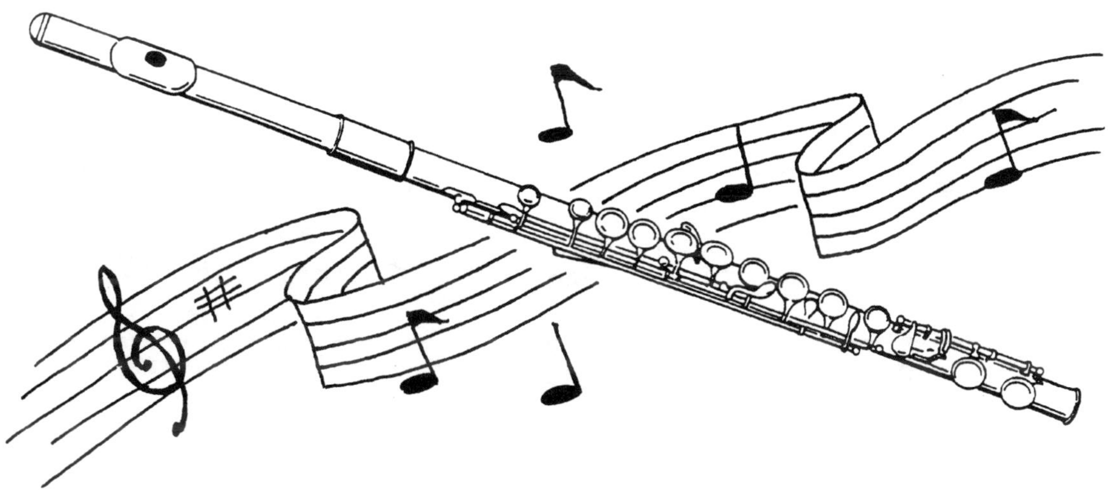

I hear a flute, tweet, tweet, tweet.

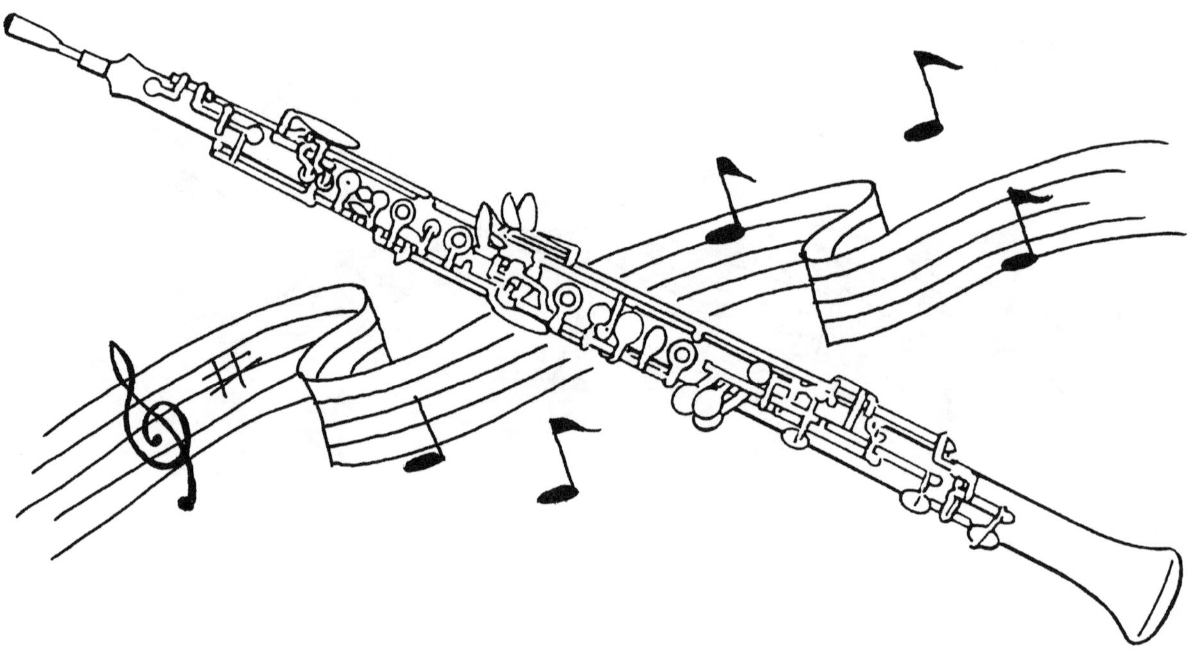

I hear an oboe, nee, nee, nee.

2.

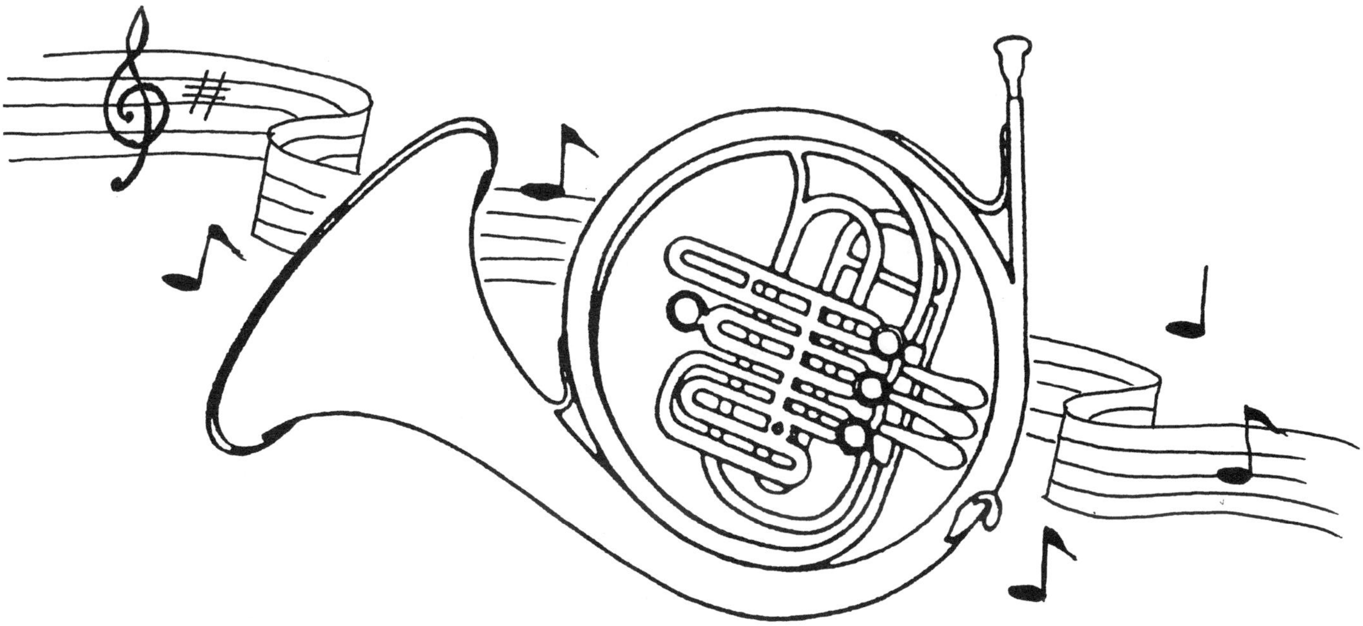

I hear a French horn, bum, ba, bum.

3.

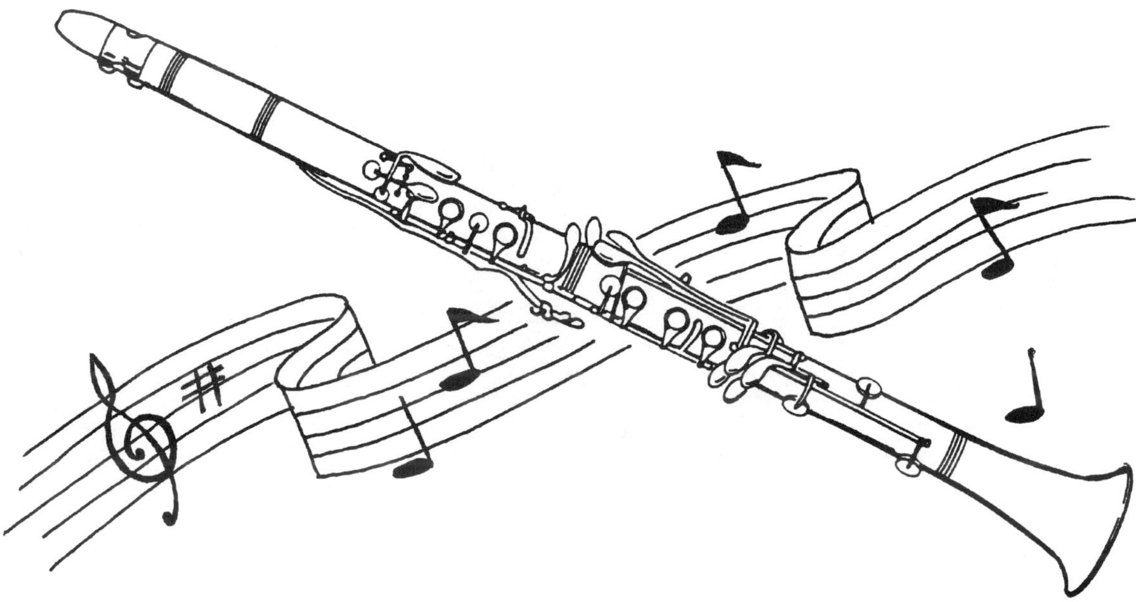

I hear a clarinet, doo, doo, doo.

5.

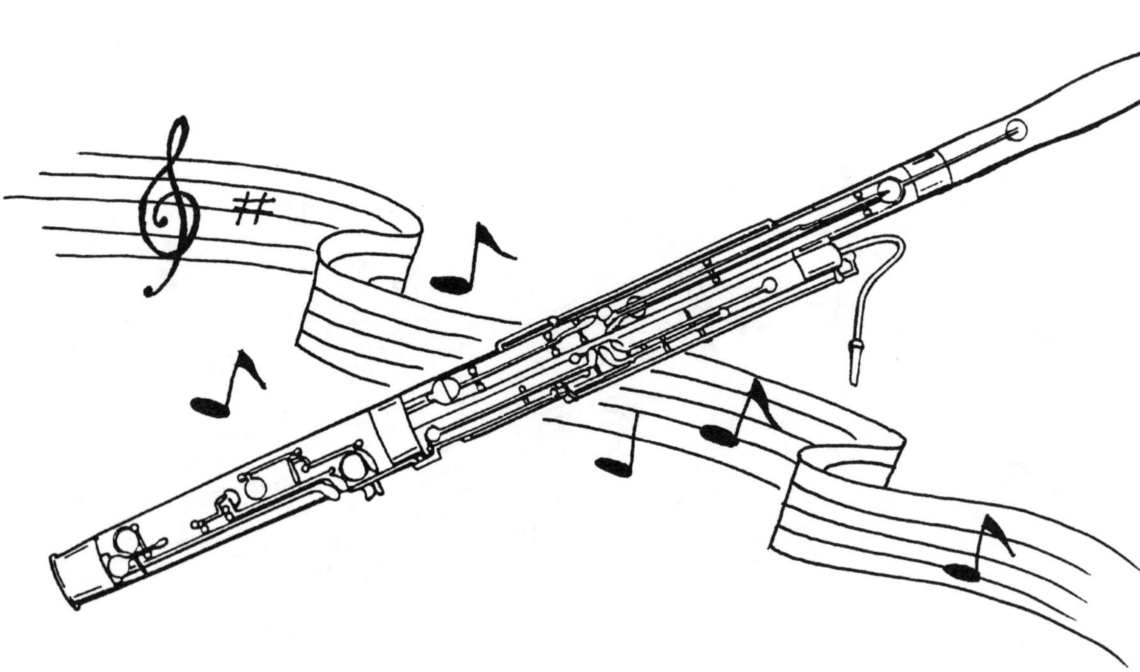

I hear a bassoon, oom, pah, pah.

4.

I hear a Wind Quintet.

6.

_________________________ would play _________________________

Name

7.

Beautiful Music

The End

______________________ would play

____

Do You Know?

Objectives

- ✦ Recognizing the major parts of the body: nose, head, mouth, hand, body, leg, and foot.
- ✦ Being exposed to a question.
- ✦ Building confidence as a reader.

Extension Activities

- ✦ After reading different versions of the Gingerbread Man, make a Venn diagram comparing the characters and the endings in each version. Make a class graph where the children pick their favorite version of the Gingerbread Man.
- ✦ Make gingerbread cookies. Decorate the gingerbread boys and girls with sprinkles, raisins, chocolate chips, candy, and icing. Before the children eat their cookies, measure to see how long the cookies are using paper clips, cubes, and/or pennies. After eating the cookie, make a class graph showing which part (head, arm, leg) of the gingerbread person the children ate first.
- ✦ Give each child a copy of the survey on page 120. Have each child ask eight friends. Have the children record their survey results to the class and compare their results with others.

Additional Sources

- *The Cajun Gingerbread Boy*
  by Berthe Amoss
  (MTC Press, 1999)

- *The Gingerbread Man*
  by Jim Aylesworth
  (Scholastic Trade, 1998)

- *The Gingerbread Baby*
  by Jan Brett
  (Putnam Publishing, 1999)

- *The Gingerbread Boy*
  by Paul Galdone
  (Clarion Books, 1983)

- *The Gingerbread Rabbit*
  by Randall Jarrel
  (Harper Collins Juvenile Books, 1996)

- *The Gingerbread Man (Hand Claps and Finger Snaps/Book and Audio)*
  by Charles Mead and Pieces of 8
  (MMB Music, 1995)

Do You Know?

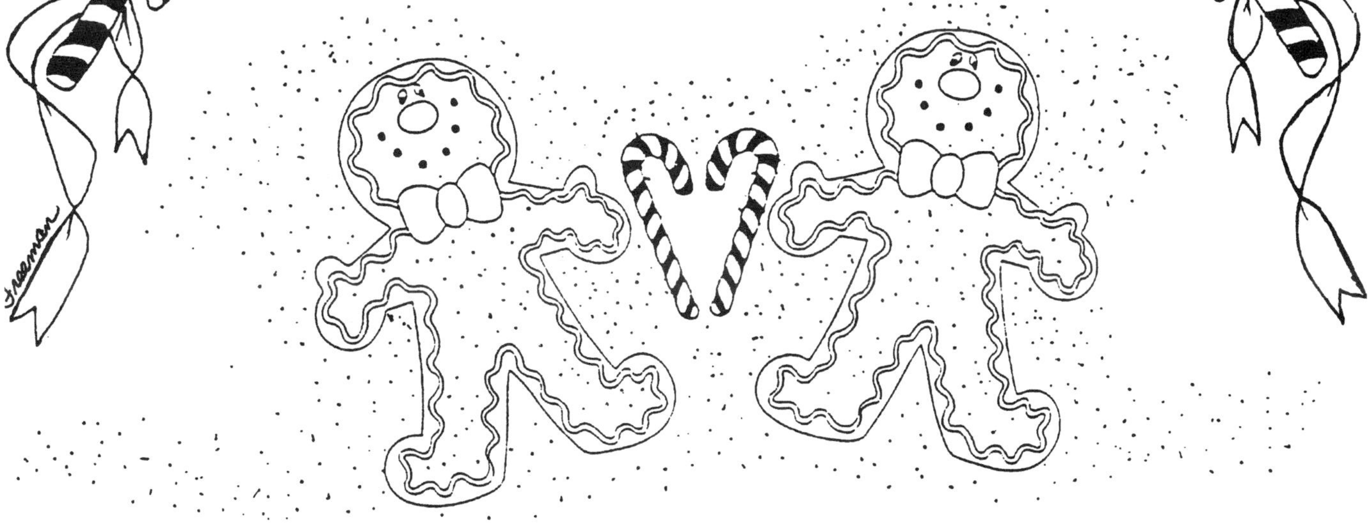

By ______________________________

2.

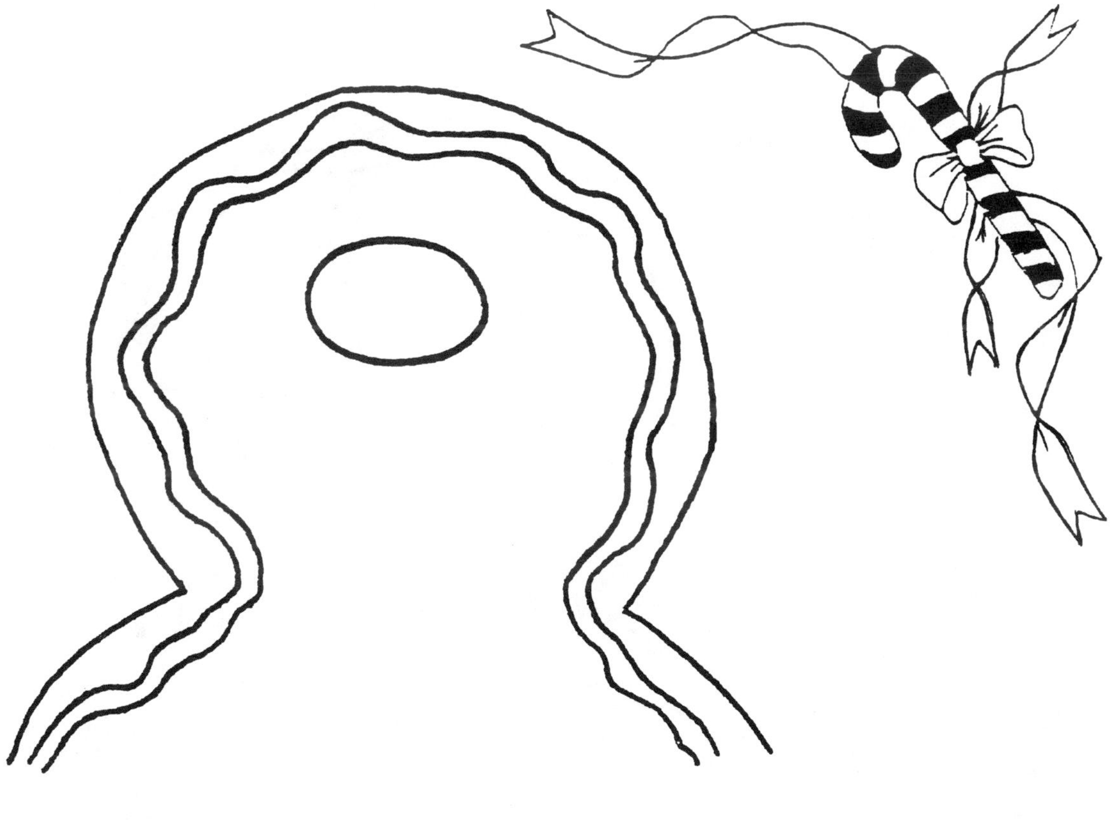

Do you know I have a ______________?

1.

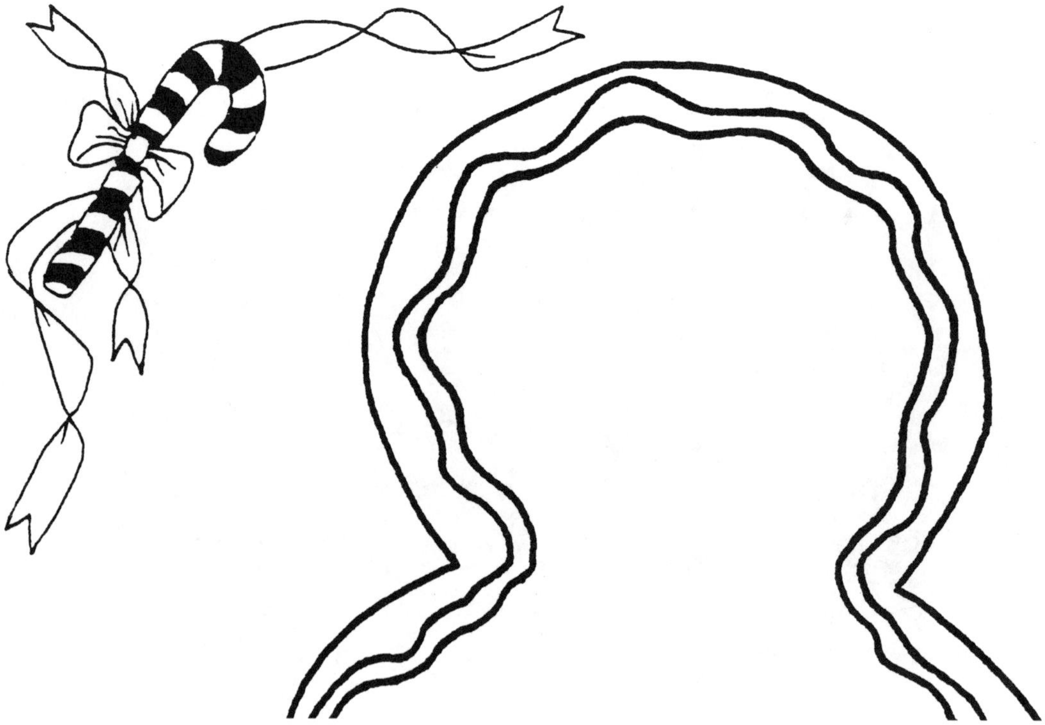

Do you know I have a ______________ ?

3.

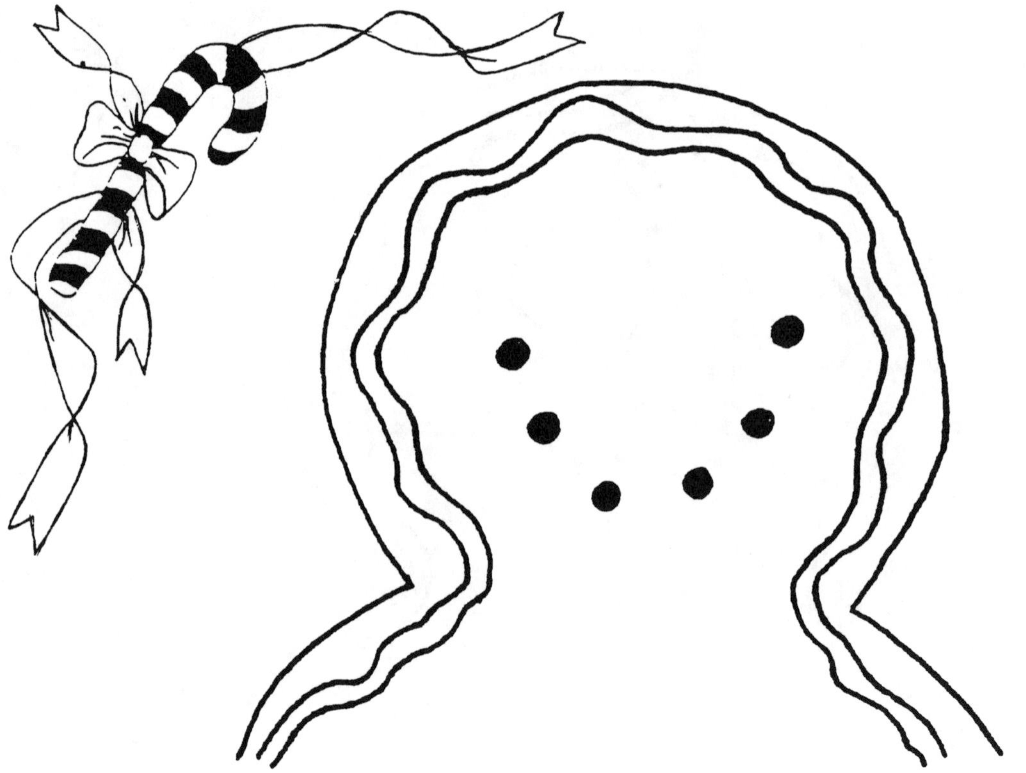

Do you know I have a ______________ ?

4.

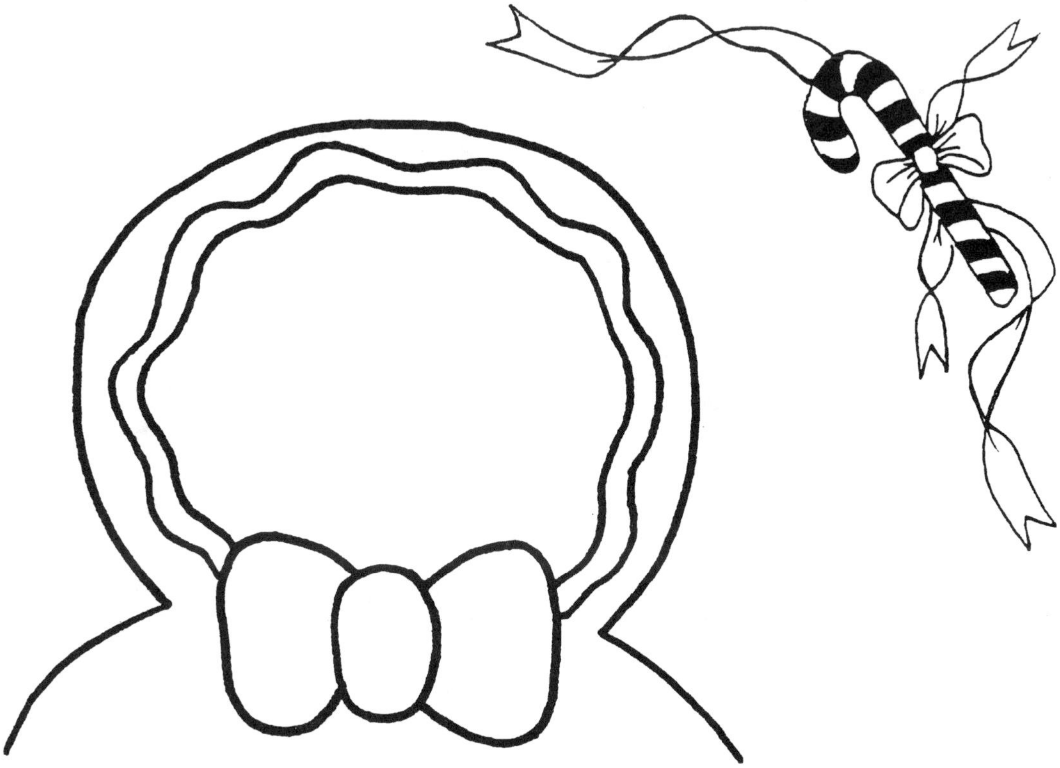

Do you know I have a ______________?

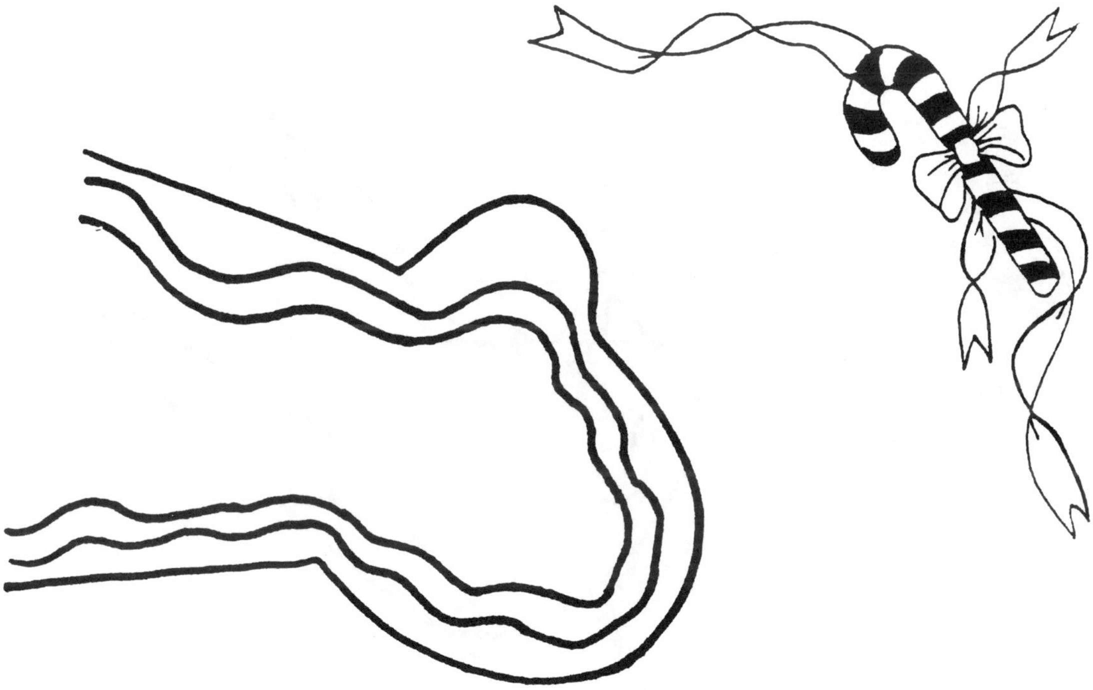

6.

Do you know I have a ______________?

5.

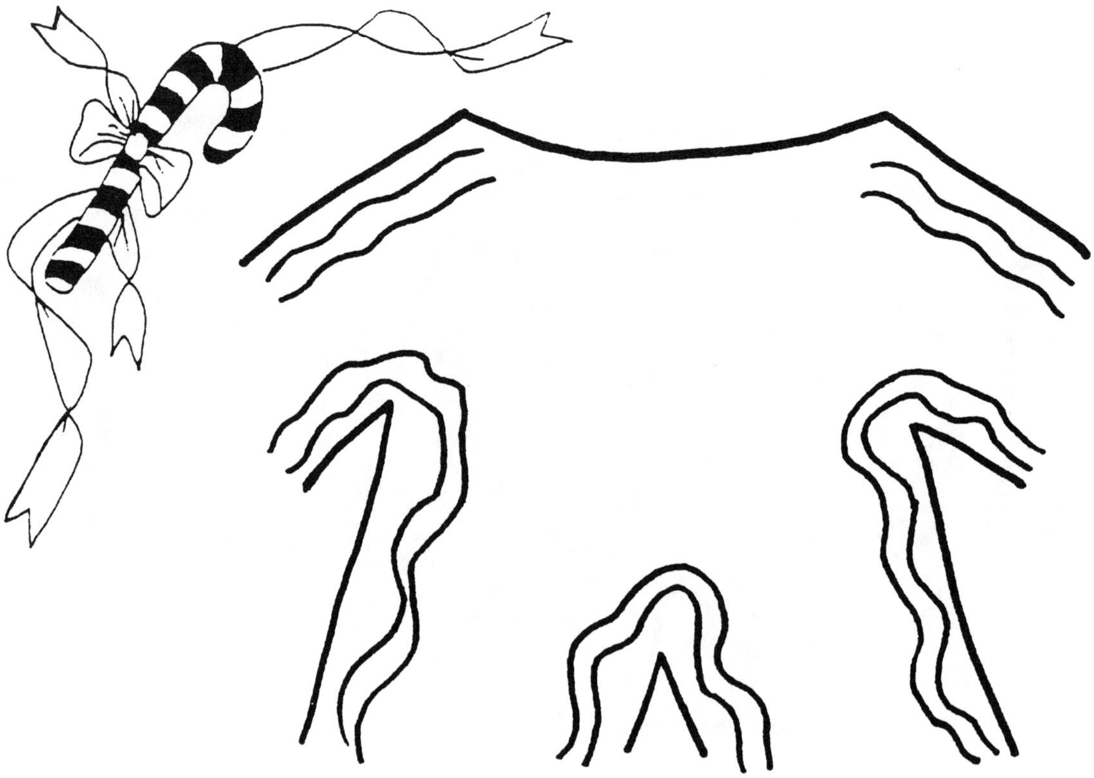

Do you know I have a ______________ ?

7.

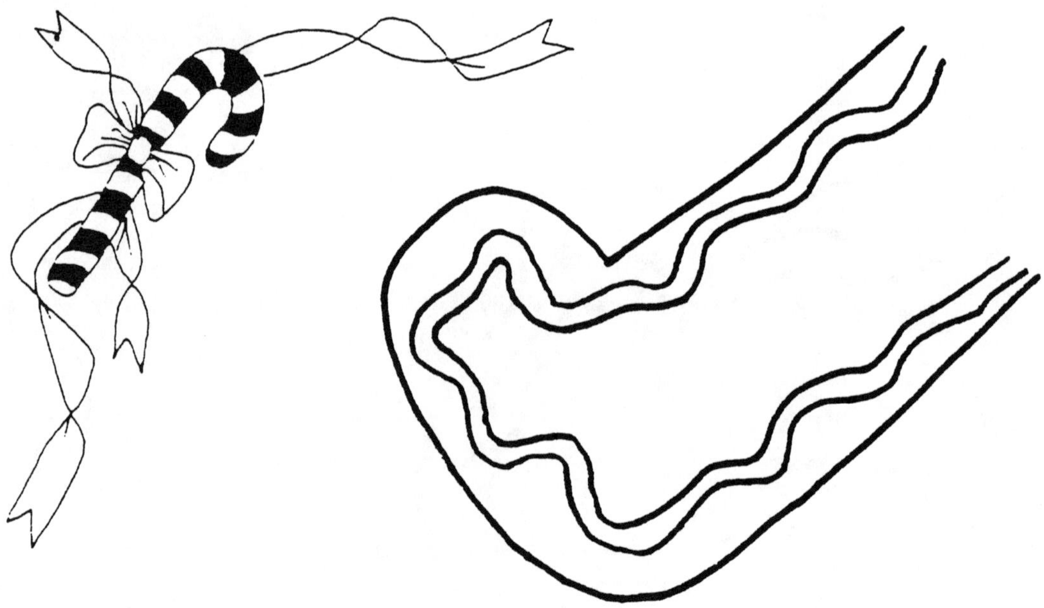

Do you know I have a ______________ ?

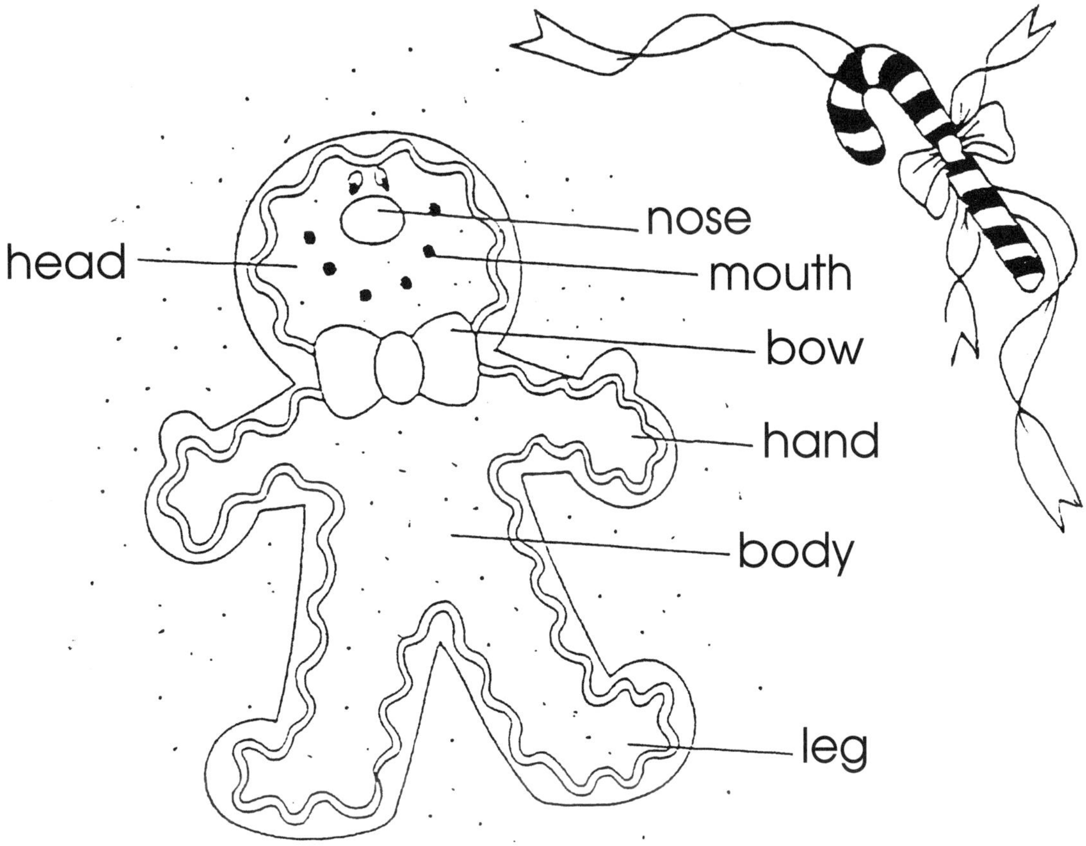

8.

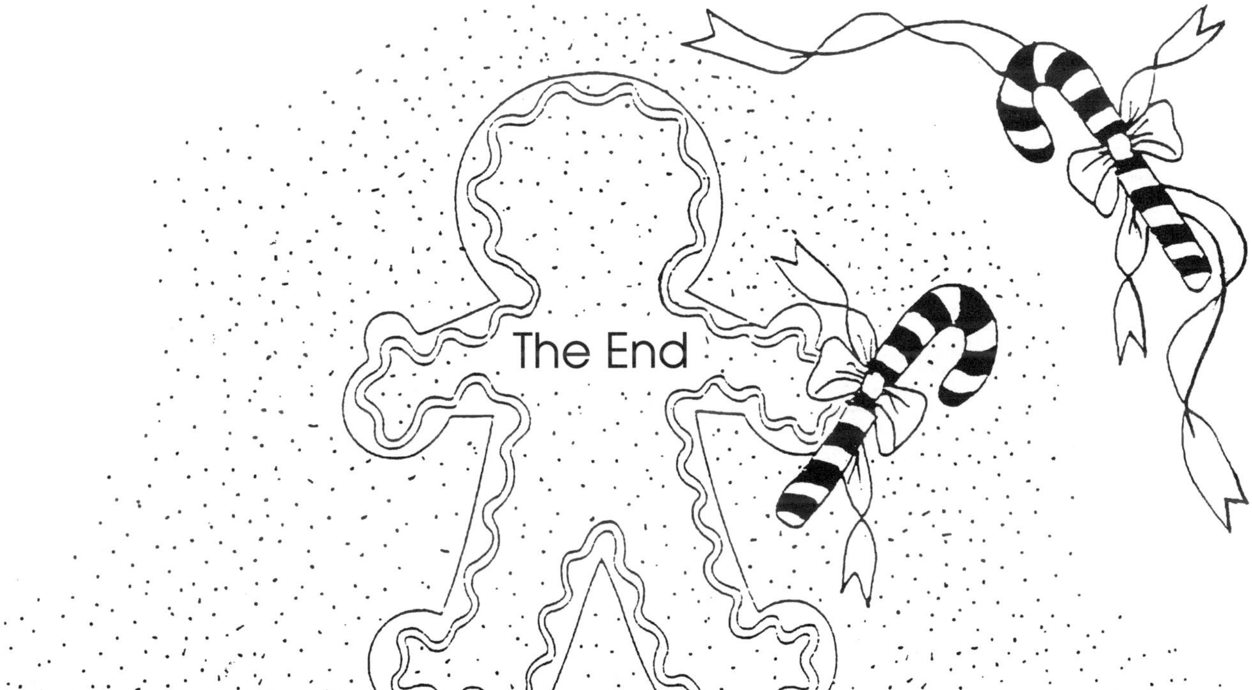

But I don't have a tail!

Gingerbread Man Story Survey

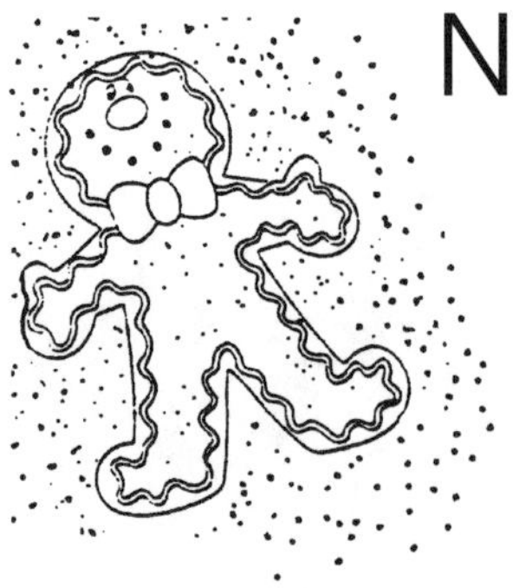

Name ____________________

Was the fox right to eat the gingerbread man?

Yes	No

My Candy Color Book

Objectives

- ✦ Recognizing the color words in context: red, orange, yellow, green, blue, purple, and brown.
- ✦ Building confidence as a reader.

Extension Activities

- ✦ Take a candy taste test where the children have the opportunity to taste the different varieties of candies. Buy bags of milk chocolate, peanut, almond, crispy, and peanut butter candies (M&M™ candies work best). After the children have tasted each variety of candy, make a class graph so the children can choose their favorite kind of candy.
- ✦ Make candy pizzas for a snack. Follow the recipe for candy pizza on page 128, or have all of the toppings available for the children and have them create their own pizza. When you have the children create their own pizza have them use the candy pizza graph on page 129 to record what they put on their candy pizza.
- ✦ Give every child a mini bag of candies. Have each child sort the bag of candies by color and record on the candy color graph on page 130 how many of each color they find. Have the children compare results with others in the class. See who had the most red candies, or the fewest green candies, etc. Have the children count to see how many candies they had in their bags and compare this data with the rest of the class.
- ✦ Give every child a copy of the candy person on pages 131 and 132. Tell the children to choose their favorite color candy and cut a circle out of construction paper. Have them glue the eyes, mouth, arms, ties, and feet to the circle to create a candy person.

Additional Sources

- *M&M™'s Counting Book*
  by Barbra B. McGrath
  (Charlesbridge Publishing, 1999)

- *More M&M™'s Brand Chocolate Candies Math*
  by Barbra B. McGrath
  (Charlesbridge Publishing, 1998)

- *Curious George Goes to a Chocolate Factory*
  by Margret Rey
  (Houghton Mifflin Company, 1998)

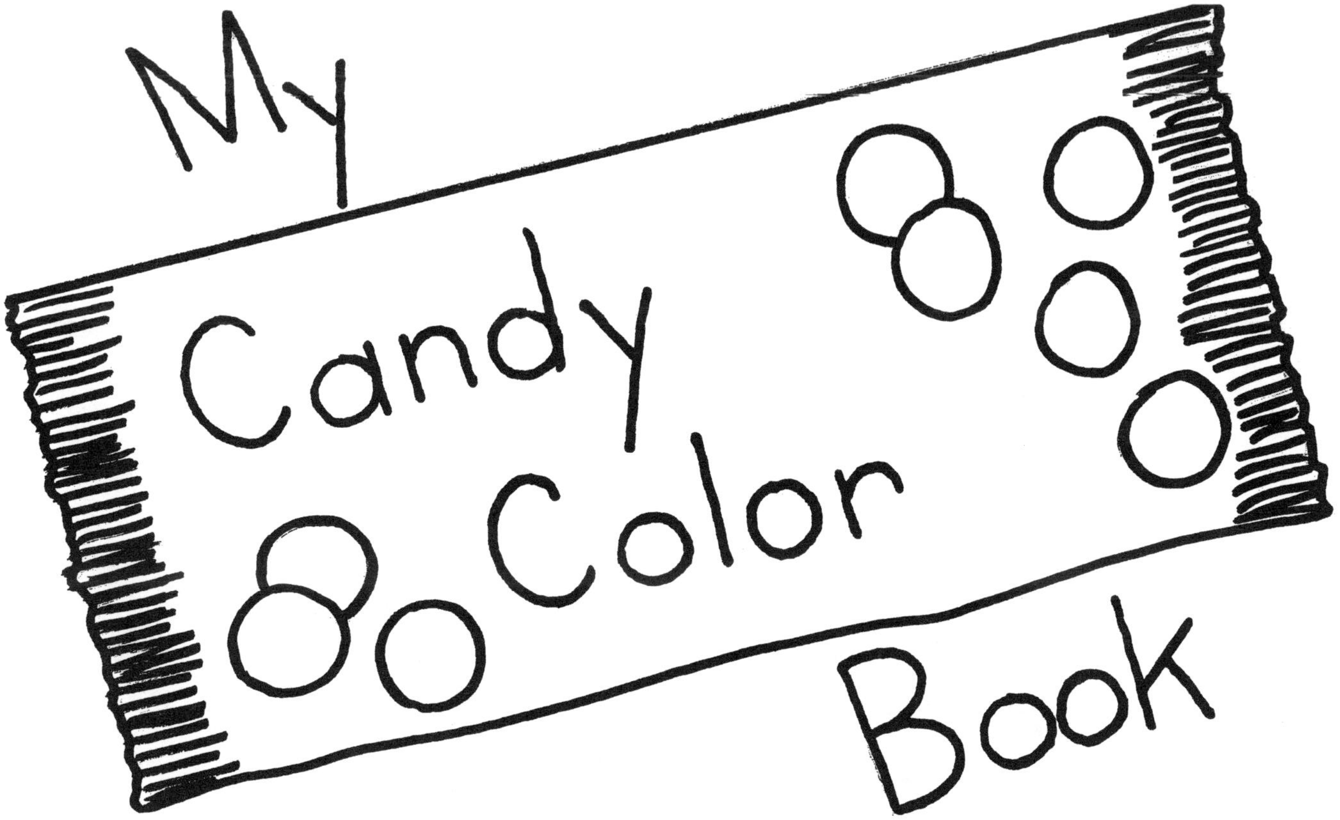

Name ______________________________

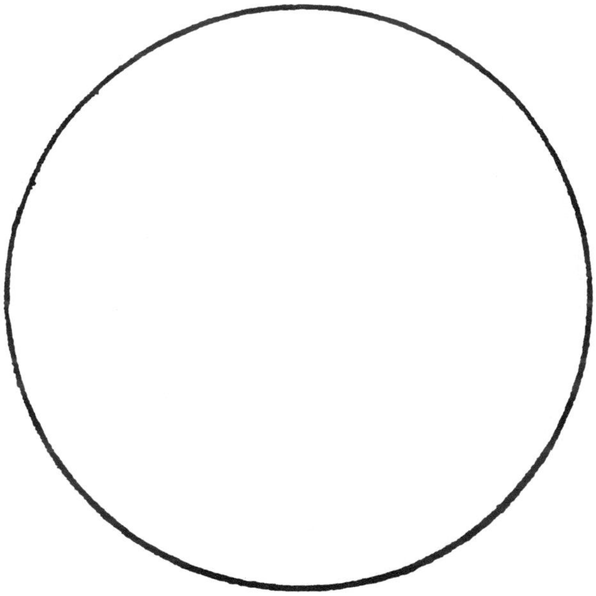

is orange.

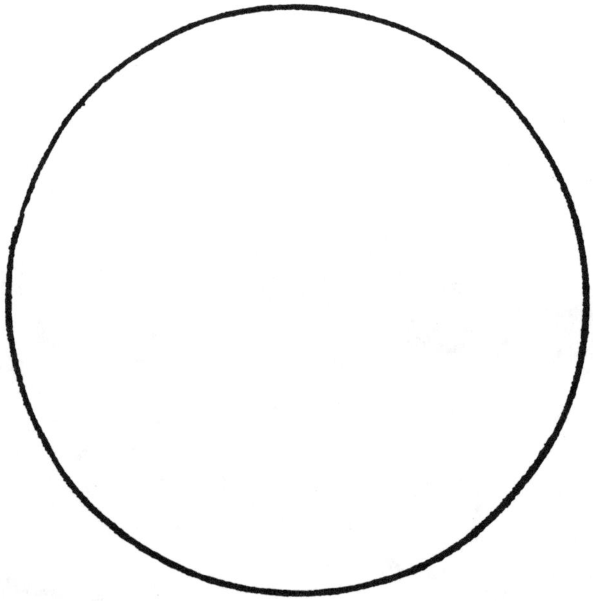

is red.

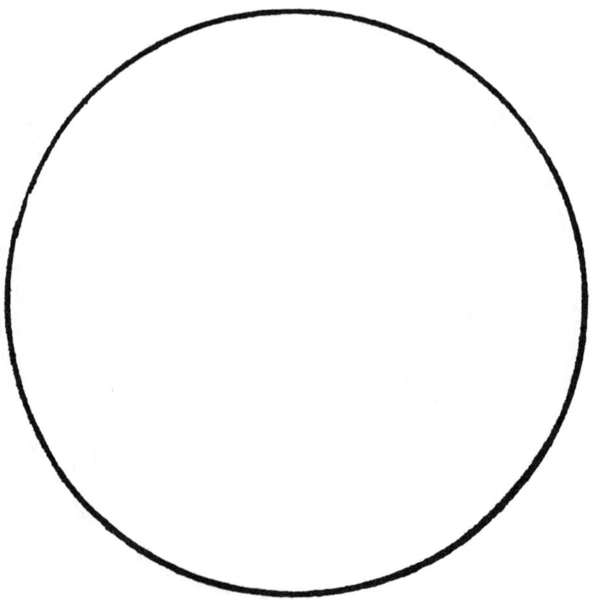

is yellow.

is blue.

is brown.

is M-mmm.

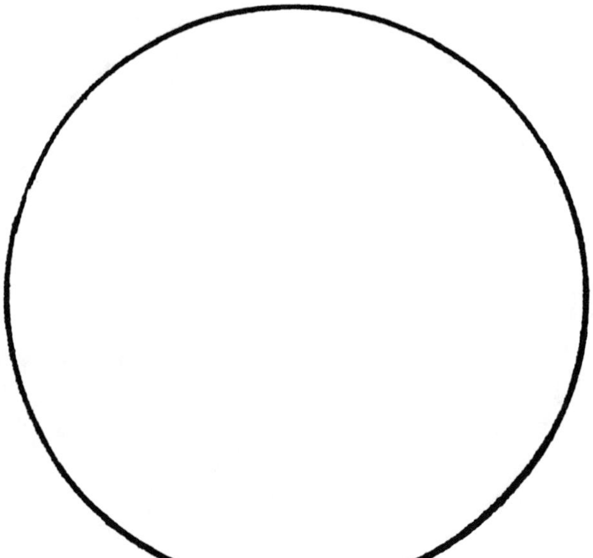

is purple.

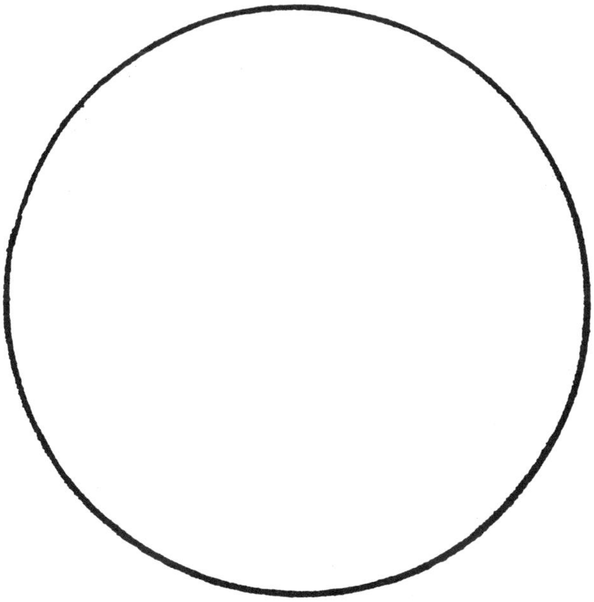

is green.

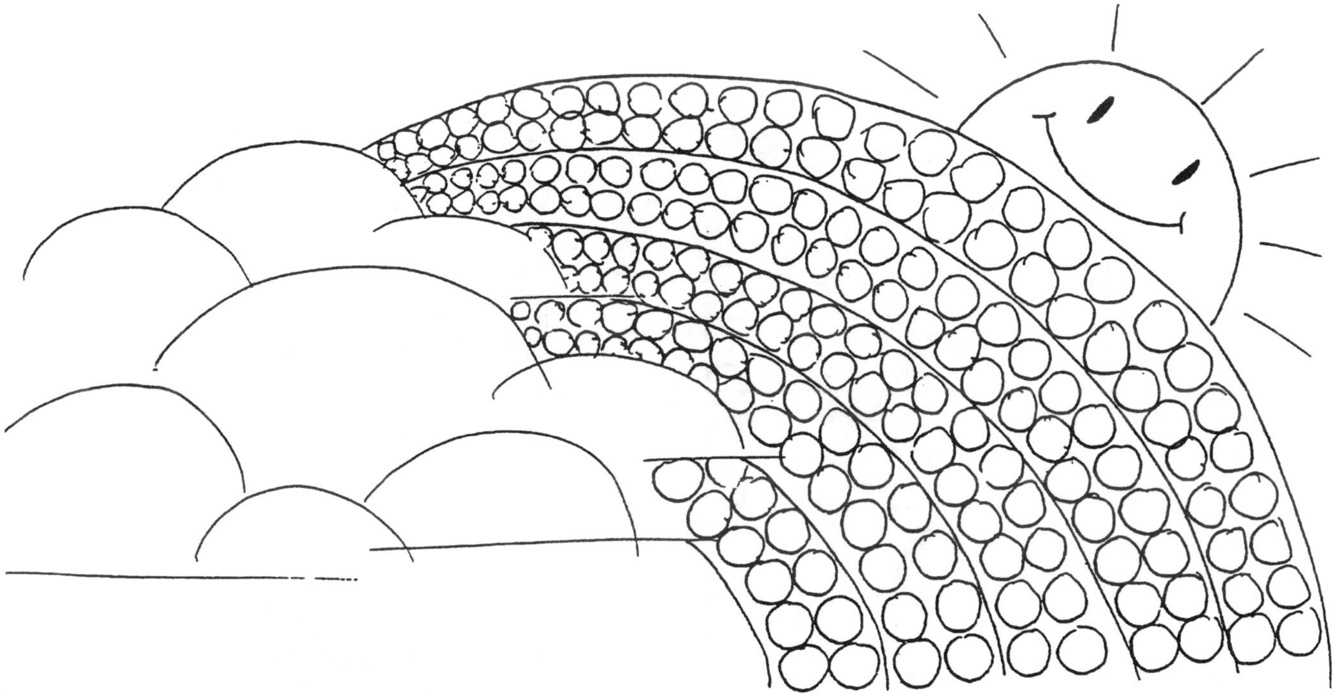

is many colors.

1 iced cookie

6 candy pieces

4 marshmallows

2 mini pretzels

3 chocolate chips

2 peanuts

3 raisins

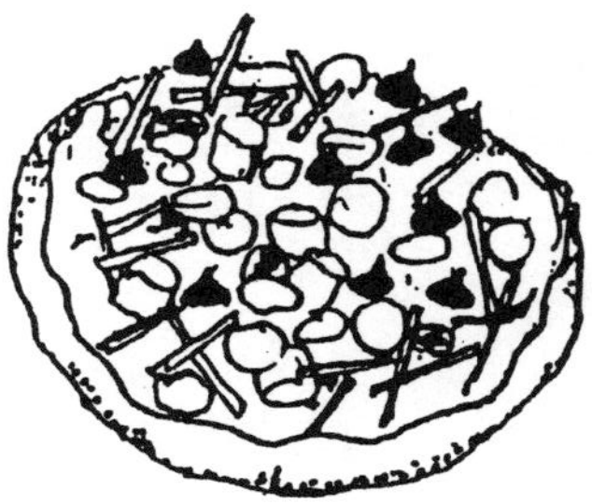

Candy Pizza Graph

What candy did you put on your pizza?

Name ______________________________

7						
6						
5						
4						
3						
2						
1						
	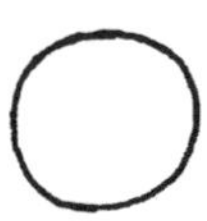					

Candy Color Graph

Name ____________________

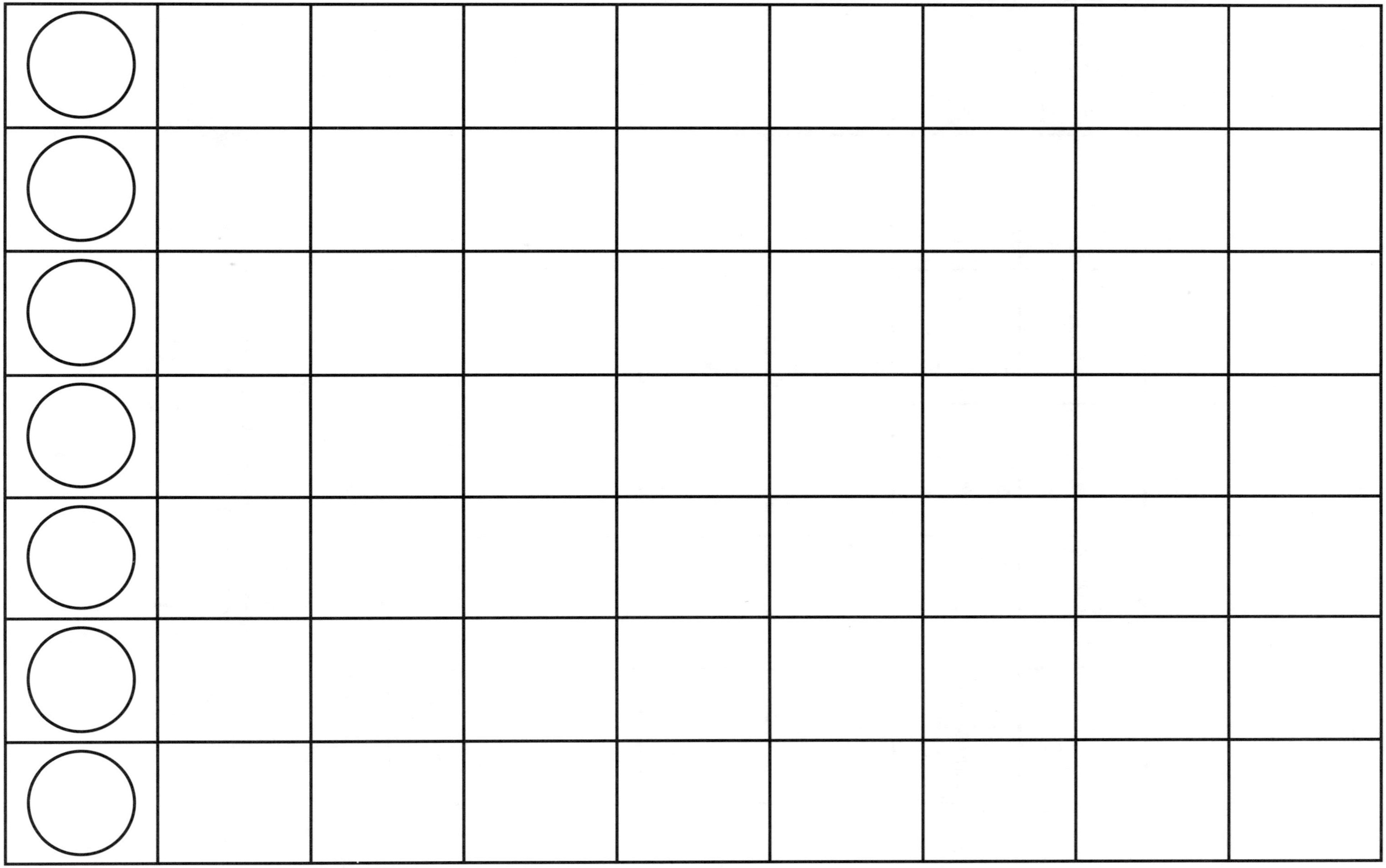

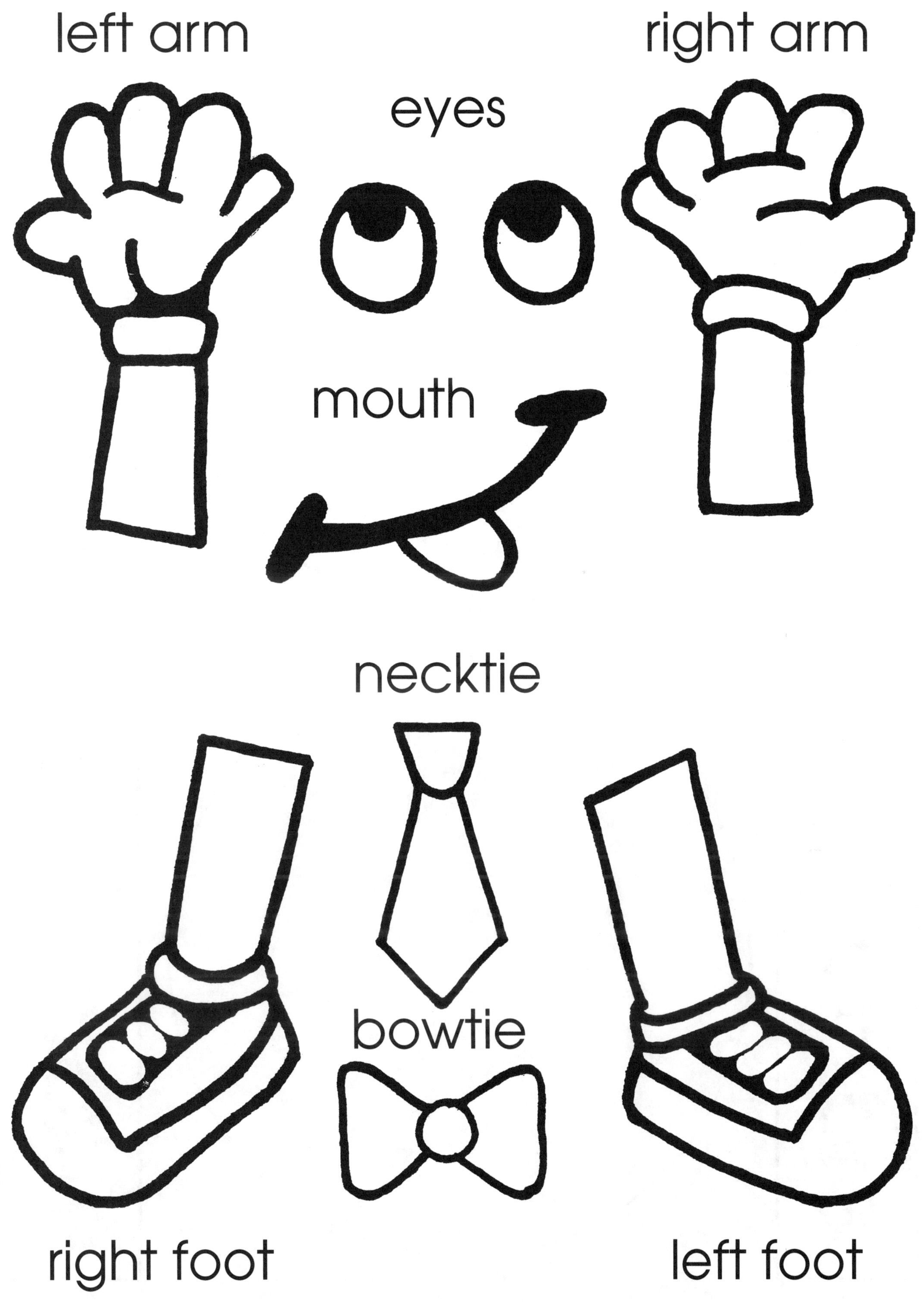
left arm
right arm
eyes
mouth
necktie
bowtie
right foot
left foot

red

blue

green

brown

orange

yellow

purple

My Domino Book

Objectives

- ✦ Recognizing and writing the numbers in context:
  one, two, three, four, five, six, seven, eight, nine, and ten.
- ✦ Connecting the number word with the number symbol.
- ✦ Building confidence as a reader.

Extension Activities

- ✦ Give each child a copy of the Domino Math worksheet on page 138 and six dominos. Have the children copy the dot patterns on the dominos onto their domino worksheet. Have the children count the dots and record the numbers on the lines. Count the total number of dots and write the number.
- ✦ Use dominos to measure classroom items. Ask the children to predict how many dominos long a crayon is. After the children make their predictions have them line up the dominos end to end and count how many dominos it took to equal the length of the crayon.
- ✦ Have the children find different ways to sort the dominos. The children could sort the dominos by placing all of the dominos with blanks together or sort the dominos by placing all of the doubles together. Children could count the dots on the dominos and place all of the dominos with the same number of dots together.
- ✦ Teach the children the basic rules on how to play a variety of domino games. Use the book *Great Book of Dominos* by Jennifer A. Kelley as a resource. The book is a wonderful guide on basic domino blocking games like Stretch, Doubles, Domino Pool, The Fortress, and Chickenfoot.

Additional Sources

- *Domino Addition*
  by Lynette Long
  (Charlesbridge Publishing, 1996)

- *Joe Can Count*
  by Jan Ormerod
  (Mulberry Books, 1993)

- *Snappy Little Numbers: Count the Numbers From 1 to 10*
  by Dugald Steer
  (Silver Dolphin, 2002)

- *Ten Black Dots*
  by Donald Crews
  (Scott Foresman, 1995)

- *Ten, Nine, Eight*
  by Molly Garrett Bang
  (Scott Foresman, 1991)

My Domino Book

By ______________

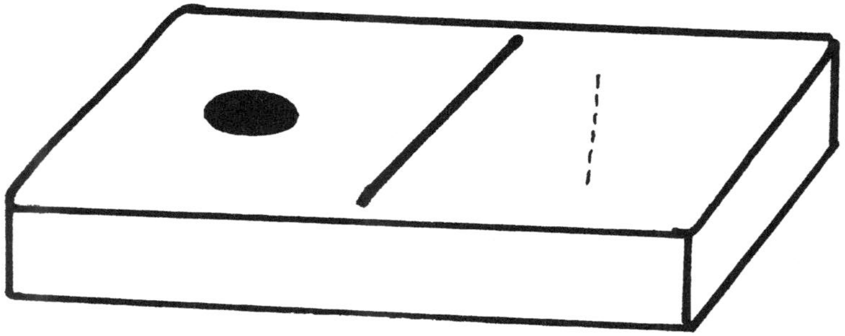

1 one ______________

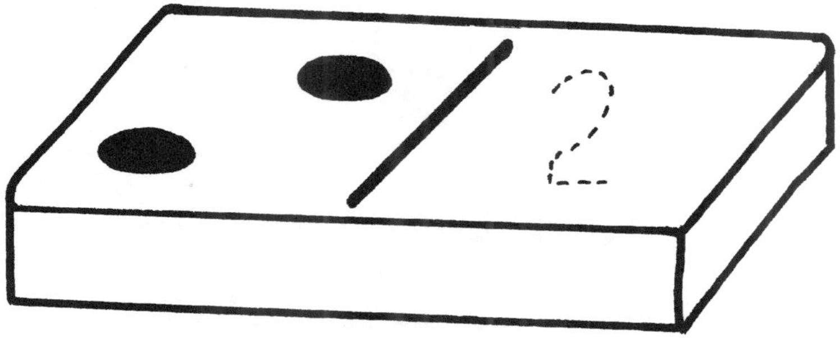

2 two ______________

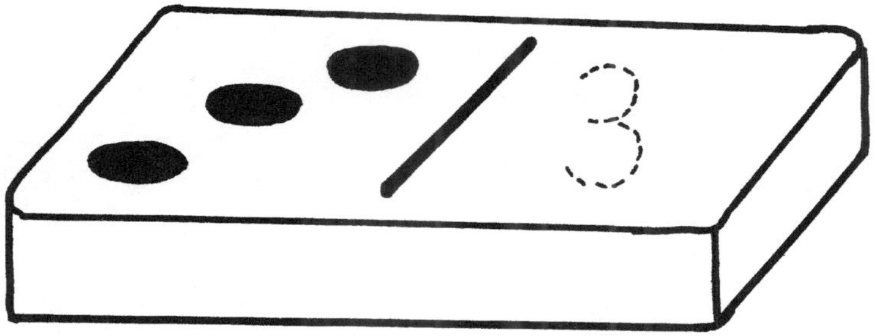

3 three ______________

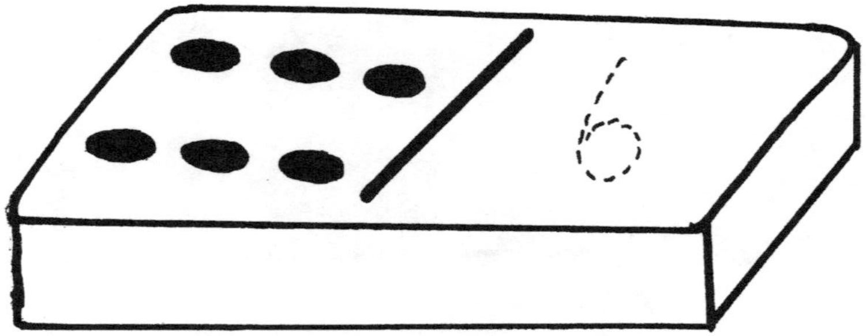

6 six

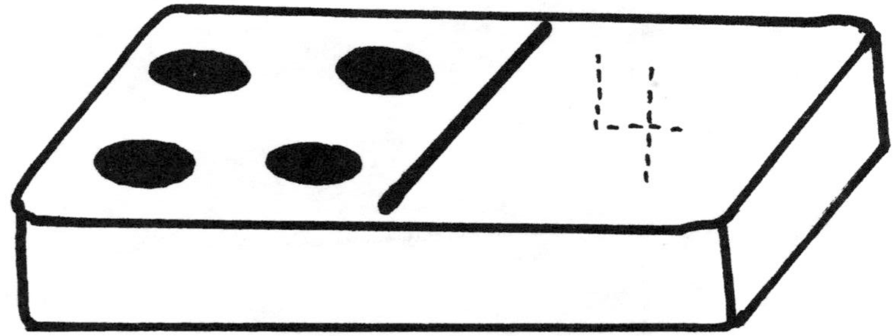

4 four

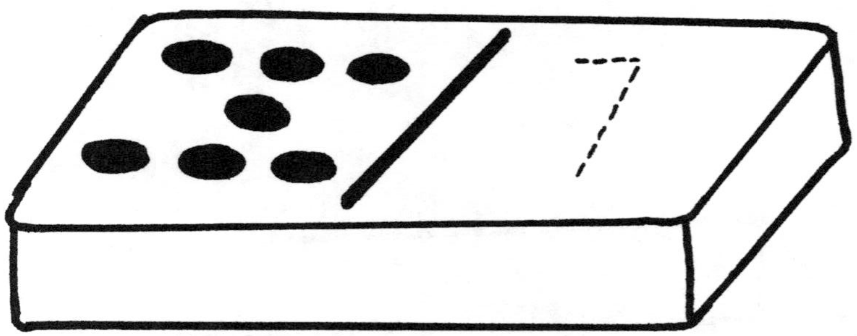

7 seven

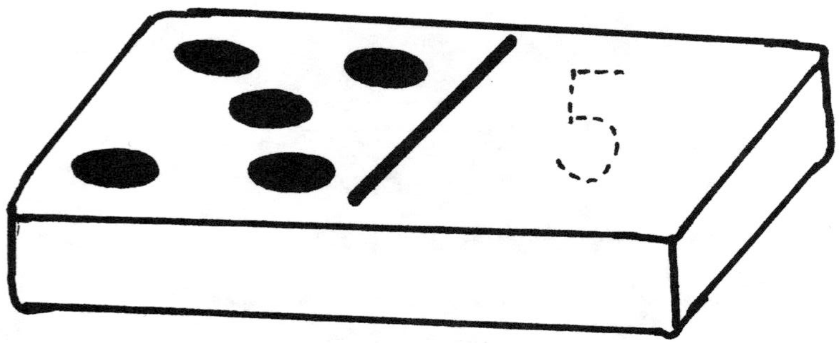

5 five

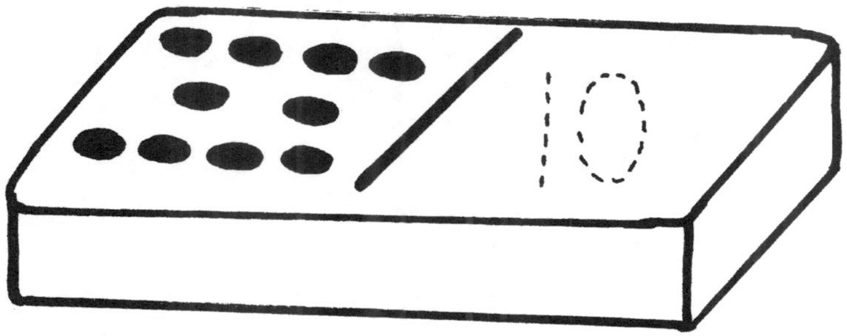

10 ten

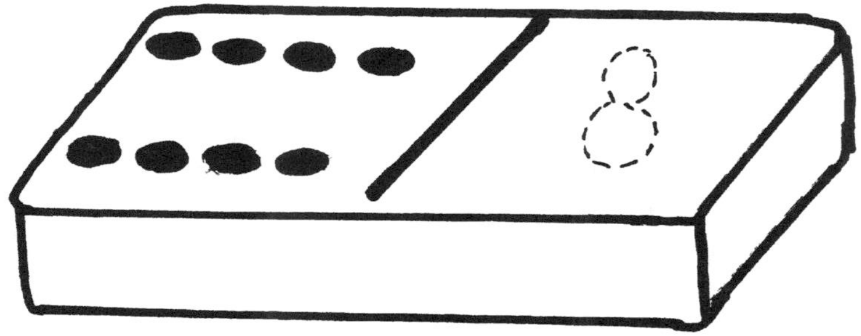

8 eight

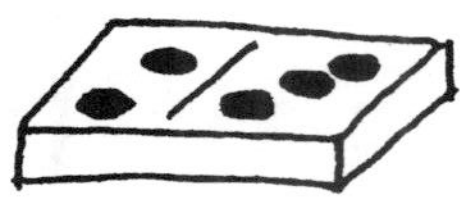

I can count to 10

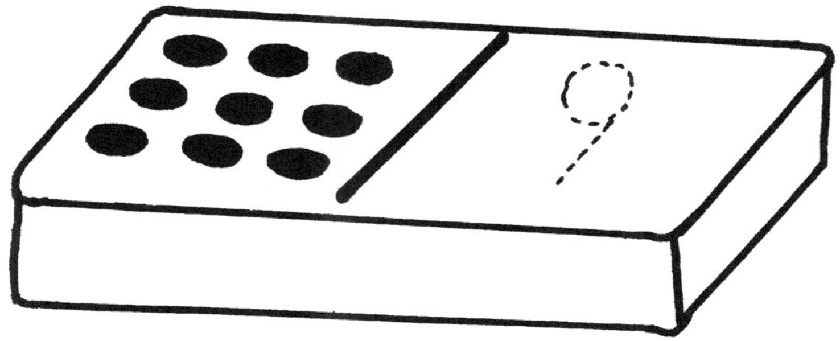

9 nine

Domino Math

Name ______________________

_____ + _____ = _____

_____ + _____ = _____

_____ + _____ = _____

_____ + _____ = _____

_____ + _____ = _____

_____ + _____ = _____

_____ + _____ = _____

Domino Math

Name ______________________

______ − ______ = ______

______ − ______ = ______

______ − ______ = ______

______ − ______ = ______

______ − ______ = ______

______ − ______ = ______

Domino Math

Name ______________________

_____ × _____ = _____

_____ × _____ = _____

_____ × _____ = _____

_____ × _____ = _____

_____ × _____ = _____

_____ × _____ = _____

Other Ideas

Use the templates provided on pages 142 and 143 of this book to help your students create additional mini books.

- ✦ My Family
- ✦ My Favorite Day
- ✦ Farm Animals
- ✦ What I Did (What I Will Do) on My Summer Vacation
- ✦ Trip to the Zoo
- ✦ The Alphabet
- ✦ Coins and Money
- ✦ My Best Friend
- ✦ My State
- ✦ Days of the Week
- ✦ Sports I Like
- ✦ Easter
- ✦ Hanukkah
- ✦ Birds
- ✦ My Hero
- ✦ Planes, Trains, and Cars
- ✦ My Favorite Toys
- ✦ My Birthday